LIVING OFF THE LAND

Essential Guide to Organic Living

Abbeydale Press

LIVING OFF THE LAND

OFF THE

LAND

Essential Guide to Organic Living

CHARLOTTE JARVIS

ISBN: 978 186147 276 2

10 9 8 7 6 5 4 3 2

Published by Abbeydale Press.
An imprint of Bookmart Limited.
Registered Number 2372865
Blaby Road, Wigston
Leicestershire LE18 4SE, England

Produced for Bookmart Limited by:
Editorial Developments,
Edgmond, Shropshire,
England

Designed by:
Chensie Chen,
Wiltshire, England

Index by:
Marie Lorimer
Indexing Services,
Harrogate, England

Printed in China

Contents

The Good Life

Fresh eggs from your own hens, vegetables from your garden, so fresh that the soil still clings to them, honey from the hive in the cut flower patch and maybe even a milking goat or a pig down the bottom of the garden. In your pantry are jams and pickles made from the surplus garden produce while the freezer is comfortably full. Dried herbs hang in the kitchen and apples are stored in a cool room. It's a lovely dream as you trudge round a hot shop, queuing at the check-out. Or is it?

Even a small plot of land can produce food for you and a large garden opens up all sorts of possibilities. Taking on extra land such as an allotment or renting a paddock gives even more choices. There is no need to wait until you win the lottery or have an unexpected windfall, you can start now on your windowsill, your patio, in your flower garden or by changing your larger garden into a more productive area.

It's not a new idea, history is full of people producing

Fresh eggs from your own hens can be more than a dream even in a small garden if you choose the right breeds of poultry.

Keeping bees is both an urban and country pursuit, while jam making with fruit from your own trees or from hedgerows is possible wherever you live.

Planning the space available means you can have eggs from your hens, vegetables and even flowers all the year round.

By planting different varieties of vegetables and protecting them from pests, even on a small-scale you can ensure that you always have seasonal vegetables throughout the year.

some or all of their food on small or larger plots of land. Today, if anything, there are even more opportunities as seed companies develop vegetables that are ideally suited for a life in a large plot and poultry keepers can choose from a range of hen housing ideally suited to the garden. Green is definitely the 'new black', with people thinking seriously about their carbon footprint, reducing food miles, shopping locally and their food choices – local, seasonal, fair trade or organic perhaps. But what could be greener than actually producing some of your own food?

But how do you take the first steps, what choices do you actually have and how do you choose? What do you need to get started and how do you plan for the future? There are a lot of considerations and the amount of land and the time you can devote to it are probably the first things to think about. But everyone, even with a tiny plot, can do something towards growing for their table and the only thing holding you back is taking the first steps. In this book you will get ideas for what you can do with the land you have and also some inspiration for the future. Starting small to get confidence and then working towards more ambitious plans. It's the beginning of a lifetime journey and who knows where it will take you? It might just be a gentle stroll resulting in some fresh salad on your plate or it might roller coast you into a whole new way of life, learning skills that you never thought possible. Who knows? All you need to do is to take the first step and turn the pages......

Once upon a time

Growing food for the family was not an option throughout much of history – with low wages and large families, the veg plot and domestic livestock were essential to everyday life.

In many countries this is still the case and that's why bad weather really affects these subsistence farmers as they rely on what they can produce. In the mid-1500s England's Thomas Tusser, a scholar and a courtier who later became a farmer, wrote a rhymed calendar of the farmer's year, "Five hundredth goode pointes of husbandrie", much of which rings true today. In December he tells us "If frost doe continue, take this for

a lawe, the strawberries looke to be covered with strawe". William Cobbett, journalist and politician, wrote his Cottage Economy in the 1820s, an early handbook for 'grow your own'. His comment on hens are as true now as they were then:

"The ailments of fowls are numerous but they would seldom be seen, if the proper care were taken. It is useless to talk of remedies in a case where you have

The kitchen garden today has the benefit of many modern methods but fundamentally is the same as ever - a productive plot for household use.

complete power to prevent the evil. If well fed, and left perfectly clean, fowls will seldom be sick."

Between 1750 and 1860 much common land was lost to country people as the Enclosure Acts took force and as the industrial revolution in the western world followed the so-called agricultural revolution, more and more people were encouraged into cities to find work. For many, the direct link between growing and eating was broken, with few workers having enough space to raise so much as a potted plant. The emphasis then shifted to earning sufficient to buy every meal. Meanwhile, new settlers in Australia, many of whom had come from penal backgrounds, had to be able to feed themselves in order to survive, while those questing for land on the wagon trains to the American West and Canadian prairies were self-sufficient and innovative in their skills. Despite the substantial increase in city dwellers though, in the early 1900s much of the western world still lived a very rural existence where it was possible to make a living from a few acres.

In 1910, The Smallholder magazine was launched and was immediately very popular. In June of that year,

Years ago not only horses cultivated the land but also oxen and donkeys while human power was also important.

With the arrival of the tractor, larger areas could be cultivated in a shorter time but working horses were still on some farms as late as the nineteen sixties.

meat bird, but unlike today's commercial farming, there was also an emphasis on utility breeds, those producing meat and eggs. Land everywhere was utilized and in Poultry and Poultry Husbandry 1933, there is a delightful picture of ducks in a London garden near Crystal Palace.

With the outbreak of the Second World War, the emphasis again returned to making every inch of land productive with suburban gardens being dug over to vegetables and even parks being brought into production. The slogan, "Dig for Victory" underlined the nation's desire to contribute to home food production. With rationing continuing after the war, farming had to find ways to increase yields and mechanization rapidly replaced horses, changing the face of the countryside from a patchwork of small fields to larger fields, enabling ever bigger machinery to manoeuvre efficiently. The swinging sixties, with the emergence of industrial-scale farming, battery hens, intensive pig farms and ever larger machinery, heralded the cheap food age, with imports too making their contribution. The emphasis shifted to consumerism and by the seventies the old Smallholder magazine had gone and it was almost impossible to buy poultry or goat equipment on a small scale. But some farsighted individuals had kept the old skills alive and were even sourcing smallholder supplies. In 1973, John and Sally Seymour published the inspirational classic, The

the letters to the editor featured a missive from a William Pritchard which was headed, "The Beginner's Joy" and began, "I am not a smallholder myself, but in a way, again I am, because I have begun keeping poultry on a small scale and my stock is increasing." In that year there were articles on how to lay out two acres in crops and Mr F Todd was advised on how to start a fruit, bee and poultry farm and encouragingly told that his expectations were 'quite modest' and that given hard work, he could expect more. Then, a few years later, the First World War started and life was changed for everyone. Growing crops for home production and raising livestock played a key part when exports were much reduced and the rising use of machinery cut down on the number of people required on a farm – although by today's standards it was still very labour intensive.

After the war, people still grew vegetables and kept chickens, ducks and geese. The period between the wars was one of the most fertile for poultry keeping and the development of breeds, many of which have played a big part in today's commercial poultry industry. The race was on to produce the highest layer and the best

Even back in 1910, many people thought of themselves as smallholders despite only having a small amount of land because they kept a few chickens.

A poster, for the U.S. Department of Agriculture, promoting victory gardens and showing vegetables to grow yourself during the war years.

During the war it was vital for everyone to grow some of their own food and many pamphlets were published telling people how to cultivate their plot

In wartime, women who had no rural experience, volunteered to keep farms going and learnt valuable skills as a result.

People found they could grow a range of vegetables in their backyard or even in pots or windowsills. Beans, for example, grow upwards and take up less space.

Complete Book of Self-Sufficiency, clearly subtitled, 'The science and art of producing and preserving your own food". The plus point was that the authors "haven't only read about it – they have done it'. In 1975-1978, Tom and Barbara Good hit British screens in The Good Life where they converted a suburban garden to self-sufficiency. It was an absolute shock to many viewers who had lost touch with 'hands-on livestock' but was immensely popular, giving hope to many new smallholders. But it wasn't until the hard-nosed eighties had come and gone that the return to the countryside really picked up and grassroots movements in the USA, Australia and New Zealand as well as Britain gathered momentum. With the increase in urban property prices, many town dwellers who had always wanted to move to the country and live their dream did so, and a new generation of smallholders was born. As we headed into the new millennium, those who were reluctant to move or didn't have sufficient funds to buy a place in the countryside, looked around to allotments, city farms and to their own backyards, rooftops or balconies to take up smallholding, echoing Mr Pritchard in The Smallholder in 1910: "I am not a smallholder myself, but in a way, again I am". Everyone can produce something from their land and here in the twenty-first century people are keener than ever to live from the land.

Taking the first steps

So you have decided to join the long tradition of people throughout history who have been smallholders and market gardeners in the country and the town. It's time to look closely at what you need to get started.

What land do you have?

A basic question this but the first one to consider. Obviously you will know what size garden you have but can you increase its size? There are a number of ways to do this; if you have a large lawn area then you can take some or all of that for growing and make it into beds. As with anything, don't rush into it, take some and see how it goes but bear in mind that you have more available. Even a small greenhouse will increase your garden area as you can grow crops in grow-bags and containers at different levels and offer protection from the weather and from pests. If your backyard is concreted then consider installing a raised bed or two which will also make it easier to garden. By

A large, well drained garden, laid to grass and used to keep a small number of sheep. A well built shelter and plenty of hedging protect from the weather.

choosing vegetables that do well in pots and containers, you can produce crops and be able to really keep an eye on them. And don't forget 'vertical gardening'. Hanging baskets don't have to have flowers, they can be great for strawberries, herbs or tomatoes for example. You can grow vegetables that climb such as runner beans and they will take up less space. Fruit trees can be pruned and trained to grow upwards or to other shapes that will allow them to bear fruit but take up less room. Cordons, for example, are single-stemmed trees with fruiting spurs planted at an angle. They take less space and crop earlier than most other forms which means that more varieties can be got into a small space. So although your land area may remain the same, by careful planning you can use every inch.

It's quite possible to keep poultry in small gardens if

A much smaller garden makes use of hanging baskets to provide juicy, fresh tomatoes throughout the summer for the family.

A mature apple tree gives fruit in abundance and offers choices of making and freezing pies, preserving as chutney or pickle and even making cider plus storing whole fruits through the winter.

Geese need grass and an area to range - they don't care if it is in the countryside or the town!

you choose the breeds carefully and provide correct housing which is kept very clean. You may have land being used as an orchard or a play area, some of which could be given over to livestock keeping or you might be able to rent some extra land in your village.

Imaginative use of everyday containers can extend a very small backyard into a productive area. Plants are happy to grow anywhere where soil conditions, water and nutrition are suitable.

A simple shed with a well built run can provide home to free range chickens that is fox and dog proof.

Where do you live?

If you live in a built-up area then keeping livestock becomes more of a challenge.

Neighbours often object to the noise of poultry, even chickens clucking, so before embarking on poultry keeping you need to ensure that they will be happy with your new enterprise. You could perhaps consider keeping quail instead as they are quieter. You'll have to keep any livestock scrupulously clean with no waste food as rats will soon spot a tasty meal and both you and your neighbours will not tolerate that. If you have a small garden but no neighbours, then it's pretty much down to space alone that dictates what you keep and a decent sized shed and run would support a few good laying hens.

Type of land

The type of land will dictate what you can do. If it gets very wet then that will limit the amount of livestock you can keep and make gardening difficult. If your land is rocky that will make digging difficult and you'll need to consider alternative methods such as large containers, raised beds or making new beds. Or you'll have to choose crops accordingly such as fruit trees and bushes that don't require cultivation. Is your land on a slope? When does it get the sun?

Also look round your land carefully and note the areas of shade, the areas that are more protected from heavy rain and wind, the exposed areas and areas where perhaps adjacent plants and trees are affecting

your ground. For example, if one side backs on to a wood, the trees may take water and goodness from the soil. A ditch next to the land may cause water to drain excessively. Really look at your land, whether it is a small concreted area, a half acre garden or a couple of acres. Make a sketch of it and write everything down. If a paddock, does it have a weedy patch? Is the grass better in one place than another?

Which spot is sheltered? You'll probably need to do this over a few days at different times of the day to get an accurate picture. Only if you know exactly what land is available, can you plan to get the most from it.

Time

This is where you must be brutally honest with yourself. How much time do you really have to devote to your crops and livestock? If you don't have much time, then there is still a lot you can do – some crops even like a bit of healthy neglect! Livestock doesn't though so you need to be able to devote at least an hour a day to any sort of livestock to keep it clean, well fed and watered. That's only half an hour morning and evening but for some people on tight schedules or who have to stay away, that's still too precious to lose. And you may well have to spend longer at weekends redoing housing, moving runs, undertaking routine prevention procedures such as louse powder and carefully

Do you have fruit trees and if so are they in need of pruning or feeding to enable them to reach their full potential?

It's lovely to keep ponies as pets or even for driving but remember that their grazing area will eat into land you can use for other livestock or for growing crops.

checking for good health. Be honest about your time.

Although plants don't suffer in the way livestock does if neglected, it is miserable if you don't have enough time to pick crops or water and feed and you can see your efforts going to waste. Never take on too much to start with and be aware of how long tasks will take to accomplish. There are plenty of things that can be done with a minimum of time – salad leaves in pots by the back door, a herb garden, top fruit like apples and pears or cut-and-come-again vegetables, so choose those if time is short.

Ask yourself….
- Is my garden a backyard, a small garden, a medium garden, a large garden or a smallholding?
- How much land is realistically available?
- Can I increase the amount of land by reorganising the space?
- What is acceptable in the area I live?
- What type of soil is the land – heavy, medium, light, sandy?
- Is the land prone to flooding or to drought?

It is amazing how much produce a small but well planned greenhouse can produce all year round.

- Can the land be worked all year round or does it get too wet or too dry?
- Is the land sheltered or exposed?
- What part of the land gets the most sun?
- What part of the land is the most sheltered?
- Does anything around the land affect it, such as a woodland, a neighbour's garden, a stream, a ditch or a road?
- How much time do you have a day for routine care of your crops or livestock?
- How much time at the weekend do you have for extra care of your crops or livestock?
- Are there some parts of the year where you can find more or less time?
- Do you enjoy working outside in all weathers or are there some parts of the year you prefer?
- When you have the answers to all these, you'll be better able to choose the options that suit your individual situation.

Chickens in your backyard

As with all livestock, keeping them successfully is about the breeds you choose and how well you care for them. It's perfectly possible to keep poultry in even an urban situation if you plan properly.

This little bantam is very happy ranging amongst the established shrubs in this small garden but keep young and tender plants away from him.

Look carefully at your garden for an area that would lend itself to a chicken run such as this sheltered spot that even includes some shady trees.

With over 100 pure breed poultry breeds including miniatures, bantams and large fowl, there is a wealth of choice for every situation.   Add to this the hybrid hens which are increasing in choice, including those specifically for outdoor free range situations, and choosing the birds becomes a delightful occupation.

Having evaluated the amount of land you have available you will already know if you want to keep smaller birds (bantams or miniatures) or the large fowl. With this in mind, first you need to think about what poultry need. Although obviously the larger the bird, the more space it needs, all poultry require similar equipment and care.

A solidly constructed house and run but one that can still be easily moved around the garden area to provide a fresh run for the bantams and pest control with fertiliser for the garden.

Bantams are an ideal choice where space is limited but they still need to be able to move around and to scratch - something all poultry enjoys.

What do chickens need?

Pay attention to the three 'F's – Fencing, Foxes and Food.

Fencing

To sum up – keeping poultry in and keeping predators out.

Keeping hens in is probably a lot easier than keeping predators out. Although the smaller hens can usually fly very well, you can make an enclosed run or even clip their wings (cut the two primaries (flight) feathers on one side to unbalance the bird so it can't take off. Usually about half the feather is removed – be careful not to cut too near where the growing feathers have an active blood supply). The watchword for the size of the

To be able to move runs around, poultry net which is electrified is very useful. Most poultry breeds can fly so they need to have their flight feathers clipped at the top to prevent this which is a painless procedure.

Permanent fox proof fencing of a very good sized run for free range hens will ensure the safety and well being of the flock. The understocking ensures that the pasture is always fresh.

A feeder that protects the feed and allows only measured amounts out as the bird pecks discourages vermin such as rats.

Although these young fox cubs look cuddly in captivity, in the wild they are constantly on the look out for lunch - your chickens are right at the top of their list.

area is not so much, "What size do they need?" but to have a larger space than is necessary, especially if it is to be permanent and the birds are living in it all the time. For keeping predators out, first identify the threats. In some places, two-legged bipeds require strong fencing with padlocks while in others next door's dog could be a problem. Cats rarely bother with hens but some winged predators will be attracted by small bantams and there are also stoats, weasels, stray ferrets and even rats to consider. It is worth setting up a strong, well-fenced run, preferably two, so that you can test one right at the beginning so you know your poultry will be safe. If buying a run, buy a good-sized run and make sure it is strong. Electric poultry netting is efficient in some situations.

Foxes

Wherever you live, whichever country and whether in the town or country, foxes are likely to be your biggest problem. If you've never seen one in your area, when you get your chooks home, you will start to notice them. They are drawn to chickens like a magnet and

are strong and imaginative in their efforts to get a chicken dinner. Prevention is almost certainly going to be better than cure, so good fencing is your best option and scrupulous shutting up at night in a well-made house from dusk to dawn, will protect them. You can buy electric automatic pop-hole closers if work times make it difficult to do this.

Food

Poultry do not live on scraps and in some countries even vegetable kitchen scraps are forbidden. But luckily there are many excellent poultry feeds that provide a balanced ration, including calcium to help make the egg shell. Usually they come as chick crumbs, grower's pellets and then a choice between layers pellets and mash. Pellets are the most usual choice though some poultry keepers believe dry mash keeps poultry busy longer and thus helps to avoid feather pecking. In addition you can also get specialist rations such as "Fancy Bantam" or a "Garden Mix". Whichever you choose, it will provide vitamins and minerals as well as the necessary nutrition. As a hen is born with the capacity to lay a certain number of eggs, it is your duty to feed her so she can make as many of these as possible. How you feed is important – use specially designed containers and have too many rather than too few so shy feeders can eat. Most people like to feed "ad lib" but you don't want uneaten food getting wet or spoiled: waste food will attract rats and other vermin. Chickens love corn – wheat and maize not barley – and you can throw them some handfuls in the afternoon, after they have eaten their balanced ration.

Poultry pellets are a correctly balanced ration which will enable the hen to lay her maximum amount of eggs. They contain the ideal ratio of protein and carbohydrates plus a full spectrum of vitamins and minerals.

Containers must keep the food dry and in peak condition while allowing the hens to access them easily. You must provide sufficient containers so hens low down the pecking order can feed.

Water, Digestive System and Handling

Water

A constant supply of clean, fresh water is very important. As with feed, you need to use the correct containers that cannot be knocked over or soiled and there needs to be more than one even with a small number of chickens. Poultry have a strong pecking order and those lower down will not be allowed to drink when they want to. Eggs consist of a high proportion of water so a chicken needs constant fluid intake.

Digestive system

Unlike mammals, poultry do not urinate and defecate separately. The waste from the digestive system leaves by one exit, the cloaca, between 25–50 times a day and will show as a firm greenish-brown matter which is the faeces and a white part which is the uric acid. Over watery, blood-spotted or yellowish waste is likely to be a sign of ill health. Chickens do not have teeth and the food remains in the crop first where it is softened by

If you use open containers such as this old pig feeder, be prepared to check that it is clean at least once a day and to keep it topped up with fresh water.

Water containers need to be clean and full. Chickens tend to scratch into the water and foul it plus up turn flimsy containers. This arrangement which is off the ground keeps water in good order.

water before passing to the gizzard which grinds the food using grit picked up by the chicken for this purpose. It then passes further through the system where the digested food is absorbed as is the water needed and the rest expelled. It is important to provide grit for birds that are not free ranging, not oyster shell. They will help themselves to what they need.

Handling

Because a laying hen is going to produce an egg every 24 hours, her body must be handled with great care. Birds should be quietly handled, never chased and never picked up by their legs and carried upside down. As well as being frightening and uncomfortable, this could cause the egg to break inside her, causing peritonitis and death.

If you know you have to catch birds for veterinary treatment or to move them, leave them in a small space so they cannot run round and injure themselves and

A hen's body should be handled with great care especially when she is laying. Hold her close to your body with your fingers gentle separating her legs. Never crush her or hold her by her legs upside down.

then quietly get control of their legs followed swiftly by their wings so they cannot flap and injure themselves. Hold them firmly but not tightly and do not squeeze them. Have your hand and forearm under the body and your fingers gently separating the legs so that they do not crush together, with your other hand restraining the wings. If you have your birds as young birds, you can handle them right away so that they get used to you and it will make life easier. Chickens go to sleep in the dark and become easy to catch, so if you are moving some to another house, it is a good time to take them to the new house as you can get hold of them firmly but gently before they realise and take fright. There is absolutely no need to chase them around in the daytime in a large area if you plan ahead.

Pecking Order

Chickens have a strong sense of hierarchy and this is achieved by the strong chickens, to our eyes at least, bullying the weaker ones. A flock will sort out who the individuals are. It is your job to make sure that the weaker ones do not get feather pecked or attacked to the point of injury or death. Allowed to behave naturally, chickens are busy from dawn to dusk, ranging a wide area. Confined to a pen they have nothing to do so firstly the pen design needs to allow sufficient space to dust bath, stretch their wings and to get away from each other. You can do this by providing different levels so weaker birds can get up higher on perches or boxes. Hanging fresh vegetables to peck at or even some form of "toy" may also help. If the weaker bird is bleeding you will need to remove and isolate it but when you return it the problem may reoccur. If you introduce young birds to an established flock they will be pecked. It's best not to do this, especially if it is only one or two into a larger flock.

Do I need a cockerel?

No you don't unless you want to breed. Hens will lay the same number of eggs with or without a cockerel – in fact if over-harassed by a cockerel they may lay less.

A bald back usually means that the hen is being overmated either by an over active cockerel or too many male birds are kept. She might also have been pecked by other hens. She needs removing and the situation assessing.

Although very handsome, a cockerel is not needed simply to produce eggs. He is only required if you want those eggs to be fertile and hatch.

Caring for your chicken

Good daily care and an observant eye will keep your hens healthy.

Poultry need to be shut in their house at dusk and let out in the morning to keep them safe from predators unless you have very good fencing. Take the opportunity when you let them out to observe each bird and make sure it leaves the house enthusiastically. If a bird won't leave the house she might be laying or be broody but quite likely she might be ill or bullied. A healthy hen will be bright eyed with no discharge at her beak, be clean around the vent area (at the back) and unless she is moulting, display full feathers with no undue ruffling or broken skin. Her legs should be clean and free of scaly leg and she should not be scratching excessively. She should show interest in the food and be "busy", running about and pecking. If you have a cockerel, he should show interest in the hens.

The bedding will need to be cleaned out once a week and dry, fresh bedding provided at least weekly but more often if required.

A healthy hen should look alert with bright eyes, glossy feathers and no sign of discharge from eyes or beak. Her comb should be clearly red.

In the morning the hens should have fresh, clean water and if you are out for the day, sufficient to see them through until the evening. There should be grit and the feeders should hold enough to keep them occupied for the day. Look at the fencing to check it is secure. You should look in the house to collect eggs. It's a good time to hang up vegetables or weeds for them to peck at. In short, make sure they have everything they need for the day especially if you are off to work.

In the evening check again that all the hens are happy and healthy and there is no bullying or illness. Either give wheat or mixed corn "scratch feed" – throw the corn to the chickens or top up the feeders. Birds like to go to roost with a full crop. Check the drinkers. Check for eggs again. If you want to let your birds out to free range in the garden, this is a good time to do it when you are with them and they will go back to the house at night. When the birds have gone into roost, shut the pop hole.

At least once a week you will need to thoroughly clean out the house, change the bedding and check for mites. You could also handle each hen to check her weight and condition and apply louse powder if necessary or scaly leg treatment. You can scrub out the feeders and water containers and make sure all waste bedding and food is disposed of by controlled composting in a way that does not attract vermin.

It's a good idea to keep a note of the number of eggs laid: just write it on a calendar. If there is a drop in the number it may be that the hens are not well, are too hot, too crowded or beginning their moult.

Behavioural problems

Hen pecking has to be stopped immediately. The odd peck to remind the rest of the flock who is boss is fine, but a cowering, bullied hen with broken skin is not. Remove her, treat her and re-introduce with care. You might consider removing the bully for a few days when you return her and then put in the bully back later. This will alter the pecking order which should help the situation.

Young pullets explore their surroundings but as they grow watch out for bullying and pecking as it can be fatal at worst and lead to a drop in production at the least.

Egg eating is when the hens eat their own eggs. It's nearly always due to bad nest box design. Hens do peck at everything and once they find out they can break an egg and it is edible, they will continue. Nest boxes should be in a darkish place in the house and secluded – that way the rest of the flock don't easily see the eggs.

If egg eating has started then consider re-siting the nest boxes. Some people advocate putting in a china egg that won't break so that the egg eater gives up. If nothing works, you will have to eliminate the hens responsible.

Pesky parasites

Red mite is the most common and it lives in the crevices of the housing. They are hard to spot in daytime but a sort of ashy effect is caused by the faeces of the mites. Large infestations will make the bird anaemic from blood loss and even lead to death. You will see a drop in eggs as well.

Prevention strategy is to use a product on the bird especially during the summer months to kill any mites and prevent infestations in the same way that dogs and cats are kept clear of fleas.

Choose your product carefully. For red mite, move the birds for 24 hours while you treat the house thoroughly, as mites can survive water and detergent. There is also a depluming mite which is not so common. Moulting and feather pecking can often be misinterpreted as depluming mite so check carefully.

Scaly leg too, is a mite which burrows under the scales of the legs and can be very itchy. The legs become thickened as the scales lift up and severe lameness can result. It is extremely contagious so it does need treating both on welfare and infectious grounds. There are various treatments but an ointment that contains something to kill the mite has the highest success rate, although some people smother the mite with Vaseline - take veterinary advice

Worms, including roundworms and tapeworms can affect poultry. There are many excellent wormers on the market which are given in the water. Check with your vet for advice. Check for a "withdrawal" period, when you shouldn't eat the eggs. There are also successful herbal wormers on the market.

Comparing the weight of two birds - noticing a drop in weight can help identify many problems including external and internal parasites. The legs too are checked for scaly leg.

Red mite live in the crevices of poultry houses all year round and there are usually plenty of these especially in wooden houses. The house needs to be cleaned and then sprayed with a product that controls red mite.

Gently spread out the wings to look for any parasites or any sort of damage. Broken feathers could mean bullying too.

Ruffled feathers could be a sign of parasite. If the comb is red and the bird is otherwise alert it could be that the bird is simply entering the natural period of moult.

Hens are hardy creatures if well cared for but always check for obvious illness symptoms such as breathing difficulties, which can range from the severe - notifiable conditions such as avian flu or fowl pest - to a simple infection. Coccidiosis is shown by weight loss and general uncomfortable behaviour. Treatment is available from the vet.

Problems in egg laying such as inability to lay will need to be treated by a vet also. Crop and gizzard impaction are serious and must be treated – in certain circumstances an expert poultry keeper may be able to help you by showing you how to massage the crop to remove the contents, but for a hard impacted crop an operation is needed or euthanasia.

Most blockages are prevented by providing sufficient grit.

Happy housing

The size of your garden and the number and size of hens will be some of the influences when you make your decision for housing your flock.

How much space?

The actual house itself, excluding the run, should have a minimum floor area of 30 cm square (one square foot) per large fowl or 25 cms (10 square inches) per bantam. It must have adequate ventilation (if converting a shed do remember this) as breathing problems will be the result of inadequate air circulation. Poultry huddle together in winter and keep warm with feathers inside the house. They don't like to be wet but they can stand cold, dry temperatures very well. In the summer, the sun rises at 5am or earlier and unless you are going to get out of bed to let them out, remember how hot that house will get by morning – it needs to be airy but not draughty.

A mobile poultry house that can easily be moved around the garden or paddock is an excellent choice.

Examples of well ventilated poultry houses that are easy to clean because you can stand up in them.

Note that the nest box is at a height that makes it convenient to collect eggs and the entrance is large enough for big hens as is the run.

An ark was originally designed as a "fold" unit, which meant it was moved regularly onto fresh ground, allowing the poultry new land to peck. They are good for backyard poultry and great in small gardens. The big drawback is that they can easily be overcrowded. Before purchasing, be sure how many and what size poultry you are going to keep. Because of their wedge shape, there is less space to flap and run than in straight-sided houses and large fowl in particular become overcrowded. Get a larger, rather than a smaller one and if you can, let the hens out to range on a regular basis, even if only for an hour or so. Because there is only one level, those lower down the pecking order can find it hard to get away and may stay in the house, not eating or drinking properly.

There are so many designs of poultry house to choose from. You need to bear in mind, again the number and size of hens – large fowl really do take up more space – and the location of the house. Will you be siting it in a shady place, on concrete or grass, having a fixed run or being able to move it? At the most basic, a poultry house is a small shed, with ventilation and a "pop hole" or door to the run or to free range. Perches allow for roosting and nest boxes are either affixed to the side or inside in a quiet, dark corner. The variations on this can be for the house to be above the run so it is all in one, a very good system as you can move them often and the birds are able to go up to roost (nearly all hen breeds like to get up high and perch). The run needs to be a good size – give the

birds as much room as possible and don't overstock. Sometimes poultry house manufacturers are over-optimistic as to how many birds the house and or run will accommodate. Use your common sense to ensure that you get the correct sized house – think of a chicken and the space it needs to stretch its wings and to move around freely and don't accept anything that you think will result in cramped chickens.

Poultry houses are normally constructed in wood and it needs to be of a good quality so that it is waterproof and also easy to maintain with a poultry-friendly wood preservative.

Floors are sometimes slatted to allow for easy cleaning but this is strictly for night-time only – they need to be natural grass or earth or flat for daytime.

The final thought is, can you clean it out easily? A floor-level house is difficult to clean and if something is difficult then it doesn't get done so often. Look at the house and think about how easy it would be to clean, to check for mites, to collect eggs and to see how the hens behave. If it looks difficult, then go for another option. There are plenty on the market!

The poultry house needs to be able to be easily cleaned; in this one the roof can be removed to allow full access.

A traditional fold ark is designed to be moved regularly. Large fowl can be cramped in these due to the wedge shape so don't overstock.

Perches inside the house help to avoid bullying as hens can go to different levels. Water in this house is in a legged container to avoid soiling and hoppers automatically top up food and water.

A Dutch bantam is ideal for small gardens. It is a 'true' bantam, having no large fowl counterpart.

One of the most attractive bantams, the Gold Sebright is striking in appearance and is very popular with people who show poultry.

Hens for a small garden

It's possible to keep chickens within the confines of a small garden but you have to think carefully about breeds and housing.

Checklist

All new poultry keepers should

- Ensure there is nothing in your deeds or planning that prohibits the keeping of poultry.
- Consider your neighbours – are they likely to object and can you persuade them that poultry won't be a nuisance?
- Maintain cleanliness. All poultry needs to be kept clean but in an urban setting it must be spotless and there must be a plan to dispose of waste.

Owners of small gardens should also:

- Choose a relatively "quiet" breed and don't keep a cockerel – at least until you see how the hens are received.
- Choose a small, docile breed and find out about it before purchasing.

- If you are allowed to keep dogs, cats and rabbits, then keeping a few bantams properly should really not present a problem.
- Choose easy to clean, attractive housing that withstands foxes and attacks from dogs.
- Plant shrubs or build a fence to help keep down the noise from the clucking and make the housing look extra pleasant by having flowers in pots outside the house.
- Keep the rest of the garden tidy – not only will it give a better impression to the neighbours but it will help to reduce unwanted pests such as foxes or rats.

So what about the breeds?

There are over a hundred breeds of poultry including miniatures and hybrids. A miniature is the small equivalent of a large breed but not all the large fowl have a miniature equivalent. When they do, they are an exact replica of the large breed but much smaller – for example, the famous brown egg layer, the Maran, has a miniature version which weighs in at a quarter of the larger fowl as does the miniature of the well known Rhode Island Red.

A bantam, sometimes known as a "true" bantam, does not have a larger equivalent so the charming Japanese bantams and the gentle Pekins only come in a small size!

It's really worth going to a poultry exhibition or show and having a good look round the breeds – normally the exhibitors are only too happy to talk about their particular breeds and point out good and bad points to look out for.

Most breeds are "soft feathered", except for game varieties that are "hard feathered", where the feathering

This small flock of Dutch bantams have plenty of room to indulge in their busy behaviour and the clean grass helps to keep them clean and dry too.

The striking Houdan with its impressive head crest is not the ideal beginners bird despite its gentle nature and moderate egg laying ability.

is so tight that sometimes the breed naturally displays some pink skin. Frizzle feathering is now bred for and is where feathers curl. Individual breeds can be "bearded", "muffled", or "crested" and show feathered legs! There really is a huge variety to choose from in a range of beautiful colours which is why you need to do your homework and have a good look round first.

Suggestions for a small garden

The Belgian Bantam is the size of a large pigeon and comes in a variety of designs and colours and can be booted (feathery legs), bearded and crested. They include the Barbu d'Anvers (bearded and muff), the Barbu d'Uccle (bearded, muff and feather legged), the Sabelpoot (booted), and the Barbu de Watermeal (bearded and crested) and the colours are divine from porcelaine and lavender right up to the delightful millefleur. They are "true" bantams. They are truly striking to look at and capture the hearts of most who see them but they are also a gentle breed that can become very tame and have a good life expectancy. They are not good egg layers and can fly quite well so need good fencing.

Despite their decorative appearance, they are quite hardy and forage in all weathers.

The feathered legs may need care in muddy conditions or wet weather.

Plymouth Rock bantams. These are Buff, a particularly difficult colour to breed as they should be an even buff colour all over the body.

The layer of blue or green shelled eggs, the Araucana. This is Lavender though there are a range of colours including Spangled and Silver and Golden Duckwing.

The Dutch Bantam is an ideal garden bird. It has close feathering and is alert and busy but not aggressive. They come in many colours varying from black to gold. It's also a good egg layer and can produce in excess of 150 eggs a year. It can be friendly if handled early on and seems to do well in smaller areas. They are also good breeders. They fly very well so good fencing or even an aviary type environment is needed. A good beginner's bantam.

Japanese Bantam are very small (pigeon sized), short legged birds and are very at home in small spaces. It's important to make sure they can reach feeders and drinkers. They are friendly and fascinating to watch and don't damage the garden as much as longer legged breeds.

These alert Partridge silkies show off the mixture of colours in this classification. In the male, the crest must be dark orange while the two hens show a lemon and black crest which is correct.

Silkie bantams never fail to draw the eye with their barbless feathers and appealing appearance. They are docile and calm and show a range of colours.

Pekin bantams, with good reason, are often described as a puff ball on legs. They lay reasonably well, like human company and are good mothers.

Again, a wonderful range of colours and they also have a frizzle variety. Kept clean and not overcrowded will allow their unusual plumage and long tails to be seen at their best.

They are not good egg layers and are disappointing breeders even for experts so just keep them to appreciate their personality and beauty.

Pekin Bantams are great for the whole family, looking like a small puff ball on legs but with a docile, friendly character which appreciates human company. They do have feathered legs so need to be kept clean and dry. They are not bad egg layers either but they are such good broodies and so keen to be mothers that this can be a disadvantage. You need to be prepared to remove eggs daily and learn to deal with broodiness.

The Poland is a large fowl breed but has a bantam equivalent. They are not perhaps for the beginner as

they have very large crests which need to be kept clear of mites. It can also become dirty with food if overcrowded or if unsuitable feeders are used. Despite their decorative appearance they are good layers and are not known for their broodiness. They do need good protection from the weather and constant care which should be more than possible in a small garden where low numbers are kept.

The Serema Bantam is relatively new to some countries but not in Malaysia where there are said to be 2000-plus different colours. There they are judged not only for colour and shape but also for temperament which makes them ideal in small spaces. The cockerel too is not as noisy as most other breeds. Despite being the smallest of the bantams, they have presence and move around purposefully.

The Silkie bantam has a large fowl version and

Silkies also come as large fowl and should have blue earlobes. They need to be kept dry and away from mud because of their unusual plumage.

always causes a stir when seen for the first time. The feathers are like hair, they have no barbs and the bird looks furry. They cannot fly at all and they do relatively little damage in a garden, being docile and calm. Children love them and they can be very tame. They lay up to 100 eggs a year – if you can stop them going broody which they love to do, and will hatch their eggs or anyone else's. They do not want to be wet and need a dry run. The crests can become mucky if food is not fed correctly. The biggest problem they have is scaly leg which they are very prone to and it needs continual assessment and treatment. Don't buy a bird with it – a good breeder will keep on top of the problem.

Hens for a mediun garden

Size does matter!

In the medium to large sized garden, the more active bantams and the larger fowl including the wonderful egg laying hybrids can now be considered.

Checklist

- If choosing a larger poultry house, is it moveable? A fixed house may well require planning permission and also will mean that the outside run will become "fowl sick".
- Situate the house and the run so that it is not damp, does not get too hot and has some shade.
- If there is enough space you could consider having two (or more) smaller houses with different breeds.
- But don't take on too many birds to begin with: start small and grow!
- If allowed to free range for part of the day, is the fence secure so they cannot get into neighbouring gardens (remember some breeds do fly well!).
- Have you a plan for any surplus eggs?

Old English Game Bantams, although petite, do need more space than a small garden. There is a large fowl equivalent of these, but for a garden, the bantams

Red Jungle Fowl are quite rare and they are the ancestors of our domestic chickens. First domesticated in Asia, they are not for absolute beginners.

The Barnevelder which originates from Holland, is an good layer of strong coloured brown eggs. It's an active bird that enjoys ranging.

are the delightful choice. They are very busy birds, very vocal and need plenty of room despite their diminutive size. Even the hens cackle and talk all day long. Although their origin is likely to have been from fighting cocks, they are not that aggressive and live as family groups with a strong hierarchy. They are hard feathered, very tough, and come in many colours – in fact it is said that a good game bird cannot be a bad colour. The mothers are very protective and will have to be separated from the others if they have chicks as they will defend their brood quite literally to the death. They lay over 100 small eggs per season but the yolks seem to be arge in proportion. Generally, it's best to keep them separate from other breeds because they can be assertive and, having the courage of a game bird,

will fight until their opponent backs down.

They become very friendly and endearing but don't keep them in a small run as they will hate it and in time will squabble amongst each other. They often prefer corn to pellets.

The New Hampshire Red is classified as a large fowl (heavy) but is an ideal garden bird as it is docile and friendly. It was developed in the 1930s from another American breed, the Rhode Island Red. The original birds had a terrific laying potential at 250-plus eggs per

The hybrid hen comes in many colours with a range of names but she is a very productive creature, laying almost all year round if fed correctly with a quality, balanced pellet.

year but nowadays, although still good, it is more around the 150- plus level. Dual purpose, it is also good for the table. It was low in numbers but recently backyarders and exhibitors alike have recognised its beauty (a real red hen!), temperament and usefulness and the numbers have increased. It is content in a roomy run but is an excellent free ranger as well. The hens are dedicated sitters (broodies) and careful mothers. There is a bantam in this breed and this is about a quarter the size of the large fowl which is about 3 kg for a female.

The Plymouth Rock as a large fowl breed is not in reality that big. A large male will weigh in at around 3 kg. This breed is a dual-purpose breed developed in the USA in the early 1800s. Dual purpose means that it is a good egg layer (150-plus) and also suitable for the

The Cream Legbar is auto sexing, that is the male and female chicks are different colours on hatching. It also lays blue eggs.

An exhibition example of a Plymouth Rock presented to perfection. It's an easy going bird that is ideal for families with children.

table as it carries some flesh. It is also a friendly, easygoing bird making it ideal for families with children. Like all hens it likes to have space to forage but is not discontented to be confined in a large run. The colours are very striking with the Barred being particularly attractive and the Buff being a real challenge to breed. This is because it is very hard to get an even shade of Buff all over the bird's body. They do make excellent mothers and have a tendency to go broody frequently so eggs must be collected diligently. There is a bantam of this breed which is a bit under half the size with the male weighing in at around 1.3 kg.

The Barnvelder from Holland, developed in the early 1900s, is a good layer of brown eggs. The large fowl weighs around 3 kg for a female and is an attractive bird in several colours which include double-lacing pattern on the feathers. They will lay 160-plus brown eggs a year. Vigorous and healthy, they love to range but will tolerate being penned in sufficient space. They are friendly and make good family pets.

The hybrid hen is sometimes looked down on as a poor relation to the pure breed. Nothing could be further from the truth. She has been developed from

An example of a hybrid, the Maran Cuivre which is a Rhode Island Red/Maran cross. Rhodies are known for their egg laying ability while a Maran produces very dark brown eggs.

her pure bred cousins to be the best egg layer and her lightweight frame, carrying no flesh, means she can, in a commercial setting, do it on a modest amount of food. There are many varieties of hybrids, from those bred specially for free range who have attractive names such as Black Rock, Blue Bell or Ranger for example, to those bred for battery production, often simply known by the breeder's name and number. All hybrids can live in the garden if bought at point of lay but do require protection from wind and rain and a very good quality ration to help their sparse bodies pump out the high number of eggs. They are very docile and friendly, good at living in confinement but very happy to range too.

If you look after these birds well, they will more than reward with large numbers of good sized eggs – 300-plus a year. They will continue to lay well for many years and should not go broody, though you can hatch their fertile eggs under another breed of hen.

Hens for a large garden

So you have a bit more space.....

Perhaps you have a very large garden or an orchard, maybe you have a small paddock or field. Neighbours are not so close and there is more space. This opens up the choice of poultry that can be kept and here are some suggestions.

Checklist

- Foxes and other predators will come close to the house to take poultry but they are much more likely to do this when poultry are free ranging in a field. Make sure you have good protective fencing around your birds.
- Great in summer, it's less pleasant trudging through wind and rain to do birds in the winter. Make sure it is easy to get to the birds two or three times a day, whatever the weather.
- Houses in orchards can suffer with increased pests, and tree branches landing on the roof, while in fields they can be very exposed.
- If you have to carry water any distance, you will need to plan ahead for the summer by having water butts or bowsers. Be vigilant about breaking ice in winter.
- Why not keep a rare breed? Many of the breeds that are low in numbers or thought of as rare are very large fowl and good sized housing and some land is needed to keep them. It's a great idea if you do have space to consider keeping a trio of one of the rarer breeds to promote the future of that breed.
- You may need planning permission for larger houses and if you are selling eggs.

The Cochin is a very large fowl and requires space both outside and in the house. It began as a good layer but today's birds tend to be bred for exhibiton and their plumage.

A prizewinning flock of Orpingtons with their "saddles". These are designed to stop the male's sharp claws scratching through their soft feathers and damaging their skin when the birds mate.

The Buff Orpington has a profusion of soft feathers, making it appear larger than it actually is. The females weigh just over 2.5 kg but they do look big. Fondly remembered as a dual purpose (utility) bird, the modern Orpington is much larger, not as meaty and can be a very disappointing egg layer. Some strains produce around 150 eggs a season but others can be less productive and the eggs can be comparatively small. But they are beautiful, placid and gentle. There are people who keep them in confinement and owing to their docile temperament, they do quite well but ideally they need plenty of clean grass to run on and to keep those beautiful feathers in tip-top order. Do not overcrowd them in the house and if kept with other breeds, they can be easily bullied. They do not fly well.

The Orpington also comes in other colours, the White and the larger Blue and Black.

Its bantam equivalent is about a quarter of the size and of course can be kept in correspondingly less space.

The Brahma is truly large, weighing in at up to 4.1 kg for a female and 5.5 kg as a male.

Rhode Island Red is a name that is still synonymous with high egg production but they have been overtaken by hybrid breeds. Some strains are still high layers and it's best to check with the breeder.

It is profusely feathered and even has feathered legs. The feathering and the size make this an impressive looking bird but actually one that is friendly and easy to tame – to the extent that they can be bullied by other breeds. Egg laying is reasonable at about 150 eggs a year at best. They should not be confined as they need space for their size and they need dry conditions to keep all those feathers clean and at their best. They do not fly. There is a bantam and that weighs about a quarter of the large fowl. Sometimes this breed is confused with the equally feathery Cochin (which does not have a bantam although sometimes the Pekin is mistaken for such). These are also very docile and a moderate layer of up to 100 or so smallish eggs. Don't expect them to find much of their own food by foraging. The Jersey Giant was developed using breeds such as the Brahma and was developed for meat

The Leghorn is instantly recognisable by its large, flopped-over comb and was a prolific white egg layer during World War II. It is now bred in several colours - these are Exchequer.

Gold Laced Orpington cockerel shows off his colourful plumage. Orpingtons originated in the village of their name in Kent, bred by famous poultryman, William Cook in 1894.

production. It is docile and friendly and the male can reach weights of nearly 6 kg. It matures slowly and is a good layer of up to 150 eggs.

Rhode Island Red is still a name that conjures up the idea of wartime birds, laying for victory. Although today's modern breed is not such a good layer as these birds were, by pure breed standards it lays well at up to 250 light brown eggs a year. Having said that, be sure to find a "laying strain" rather than one bred for exhibition. They do like to range although are content enough kept confined. They do not make good mothers and rarely go broody. They do have a bantam.

The Sussex too had its heyday before and during the Second World War and won lots of laying trials at that time. It's still a reliable layer in the white and light colours of up to 200-250 eggs per season but it needs quality food to do this. They love to range but will live in confinement. They do like to go broody and rear chicks. Their bantam is about a quarter in size.

The Leghorn, which is instantly recognisable by its flopped-over comb in females, was also prominent before and during wartime as a prolific white egg layer. As the fashion for brown eggs took hold, this bird fell out of favour but not before their genetics had become part of the modern hybrid layer. Expect around 220 white eggs a year. This bird loves space and it loves to forage. It has a well earned reputation for being flighty and is noisy and lively. It can fly very well and will do so. They don't go broody. There is a bantam.

The Wyandotte, created in America, has been well known for its egg laying ability since the 1800s. It comes in many colours and has a bantam equivalent. It is a docile bird and happy in a large run or free ranging. It can produce up to 200 eggs a year. They are determined broodies.

The Maran and the Welsummer are two totally different looking birds, the Maran being a smart, speckled grey and the Welsummer normally being red-brown, but they are known for laying the deepest brown eggs of any breed. Buying these birds is probably the biggest problem as you need to ascertain that the bird comes from a dark brown egg laying strain and is capable of laying a reasonable number of eggs. With the Maran, there is a hybrid breed called Speckeldy which is an excellent hybrid, laying quantities of mid-brown eggs but it is sometimes cross-bred with the Maran or even sold as a Maran. The true Maran is heavier (it is a table bird in France) and the colour of the eggs are chocolate brown. Best to buy from reputable breeders so you can see the parent stock.

These birds are capable of laying between 150-200 eggs a year but often the better the colour, the fewer the eggs.

Both birds like to forage but the Maran is a better mother than the Welsummer. Both have bantam equivalents.

The Araucana has become fashionable due to its blue egg. They come in many colours but the Lavender is the most well known. It's recognisable by its face which has muffling, making it look fluffy. It can be kept penned although it does love to range. It lays around 150 eggs a year and has a bantam counterpart.

The hybrids come into their own if kept in mobile housing in a field as they love to forage and will produce large quantities of good sized eggs. Plan almost an egg a day for the first year and you won't go far wrong so if you only keep four, you can expect up to four dozen eggs a week. The cold and extreme heat plus the moult will reduce this number and throughout the year and especially throughout the moult, they will require a balanced ration, not just corn and scraps. They will also need access to plenty of fresh, clean water. A vitamin in the water at times of stress such as moulting, will also help.

The Sussex was a winner in laying trials fifty or so years ago and is still a reliable layer though often bred for looks. These point of lay Buff Sussex are certainly attractive.

The Light Sussex is perhaps the most commonly seen colour with its distinctive black collar round the shoulders. A good ranger who will also thrive in more captive situations.

Broody hens

How do you recognise a broody hen?

A hen that is about to go broody or is broody, changes her normal behaviour in preparation for the 21 days she is to spend hatching out her eggs. She will sit longer and longer on the nest and when you try to remove her she will cluck loudly (that's why a broody is known colloquially as a "clucker"), peck at the intruder and even fly towards them in an aggressive manner. She's defending her eggs. She will lose feathers along the breast and may use them to line the nest. When she does come off to feed or drink, it will be for a short time, probably very early in the morning, and she will cluck loudly and ruffle her feathers and have an air of "business". You do not have to let her go broody if you don't want to breed, and if you haven't a male, then it is a total waste of her time so she must be discouraged. If you let her go broody, think about how you will accommodate the extra females and dispose of the males (it's not enough to try and give them away as there are always surplus males) and also house and look after her and her chicks. If you can't do this, it is much kinder to take the eggs away.

A broody will lay a clutch of eggs before she sits, anything from 4 to 20. If you keep removing them on a twice daily basis, this alone will discourage her. The other thing you can do is to keep breeds that are less likely to go broody. Some breeds are perpetually

Hens will often all try to go broody on the same eggs. Multi-sitting usually results in broken eggs and dead chicks.

broody and determined to sit. If she still persists you have two choices: find her a home where her broodiness will be valued (many breeders actively look for good broodies to sit on their eggs) or try and stop her. The age-old remedy is to make her not so comfortable and so she needs to go into a pen where she cannot create a nest, preferably one with a slatted or mesh floor. Keep her confined. Feed her as usual and make sure there is water. She needs to be safe but not able to make a comfortable nest. When she is up and clucking loudly, demanding to be let out, she has come out of the state of broodiness.

So you want chicks?

If you want to encourage her to go broody, you need to make sure she is sitting somewhere safe. Don't leave her in with the rest of the flock, find her somewhere on her own. You can use pot eggs to encourage her to stay broody and transfer her eggs. She needs to be kept separate from the flock and you need to think about when the eggs hatch, as the chicks will be very small and need to be confined with her. Gaps in netting that are too small for the hen can be big enough for chicks to escape – and for predators to get in. Rats, stoats and wild birds such as crows, magpies and raptors, all enjoy a young chick. It is very important to ensure that she does not have red mite or other external parasites as it will make sitting impossible for her and she will have to get off the eggs. Delouse her before she sits or within the first week of her sitting.

The full hatch may take 48 hours or so, during which time do not disturb her. The newly hatched chicks will be fine so leave them alone. Replace her water container with one that will not allow young chicks to drown and provide chick crumbs as well as her ration. She will come off the eggs and you will hear her communicating with her brood. It is distressing when the broody leaves almost hatched eggs and they are cold. You need to dispose of them. Don't help the chicks to hatch. Keep them closely confined for the first week and warm and dry with access to water and feed and she will do the rest. After that you can allow her more space but do be careful of predators. Keep any dog well away from her at all stages, however tame.

My hen has chicks!

It happens. The hen has sat somewhere in the garden, you couldn't find her and presumed that a fox had taken her but there she is, proud mother with chicks.

Detective work is needed here. Find out where she is sitting (follow her!) and when it is dark get someone to help you with a torch and a bucket. Pick her up and get someone to hold her and then quickly scoop up the chicks into the bucket which will have straw, hay or shavings at the bottom. She will be very unhappy so this needs to be done quickly. Put the chicks into the pen you have prepared with a nice hay/straw/shavings nest and release her near them in the pen. Shut the pen and leave them to it! In the morning she will be clucking happily with them when you open up the run.

Fact File

- A hen sits for 21 days (bantams sometimes a day less)
- She needs to have access to good quality food and clean water
- When she has finished sitting, she will have lost body weight
- The hatch will take about 48 hours
- Protect her and chicks from predators
- Prevent parasites such as red mite
- If you don't want chicks, stop the broodiness
- Some breeds are more broody than others
- If eggs have started to develop because they have been sat on for a few days so the embryo begins, but then go cold, they will not continue to develop.

Hens will lay a full clutch of eggs before they begin sitting. If you remove eggs daily it will help to stop the hens becoming broody.

A broody in her broody coop protected from predators but removed from the rest of the flock.

Ducks in your backyard

Ducks do love water but not all breeds need large ponds or rivers. Many are happy with a more modest supply of water. There are all sizes of breeds to choose from – all with different characteristics.

There are many reasons for keeping ducks. They are lovely to look at and a joy to watch when in water, some breeds produce large quantities of rich eggs while others are good for the table and they are very good gardeners – if controlled!

There are domestic ducks and wildfowl. For smaller spaces, the domestic duck breeds are the most suitable – the wildfowl do need water of varying depths according to whether they are divers, dabblers or tree ducks. The colourful Mandarin and the Tufted fall into these categories which are also sometimes known as "Ornamentals". The domestic ducks include such well known names as the Aylesbury, the Khaki Campbell, the diminutive Call Duck and the upright Indian Runner and lesser known names such as the Saxony or Silver Bantam duck.

What do ducks need?

Duck keepers need to remember the three 'F's, fencing, feed and foxes as well as providing water for these aquatic birds. All ducks need to have some sort of serious splashing water and a small pond where they can float. This may only be a rigid sided paddling pool or large feed bowl about a metre in width, but the

Colourful Mandarin ducks which are classified as wildfowl or ornamentals and require specialist care. As with all wildfowl they fly very well and collections must either be pinioned or contained in an aviary type pen.

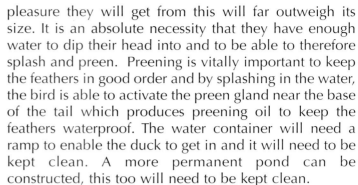

pleasure they will get from this will far outweigh its size. It is an absolute necessity that they have enough water to dip their head into and to be able to therefore splash and preen. Preening is vitally important to keep the feathers in good order and by splashing in the water, the bird is able to activate the preen gland near the base of the tail which produces preening oil to keep the feathers waterproof. The water container will need a ramp to enable the duck to get in and it will need to be kept clean. A more permanent pond can be constructed, this too will need to be kept clean.

Safety first – small children easily drown in small amounts of water so children should be kept away from any ponds.

Ducks need a balanced feed and this is best found in bagged feeds such as a duck ration and they come in various forms from duck crumbs for ducklings, to breeders pellets for ducks rearing young. They also love wheat and maize. It's recommended not to give bread to ducks, although a little as a treat will do no harm if fed wet, but don't feed mouldy bread.

Fencing and housing

Many domestic duck breeds cannot fly so fencing does not need to be too high, but to keep predators out you will need to either have an overhang or an electrified top. Predators will keep trying a fence so it is important that current runs through it all the time. To prevent predators digging their way in, the bottom strand will need to be sunk into the ground.

Housing for ducks must be strong to keep out predators and dry. A small duck breed needs a minimum of one square metre for the house alone plus much more space in the run or on free range. Windows should be wire mesh not glass and high up in the shed. The door should be large as ducks all rush out together in the mornings. It is usual to shut the ducks in at dusk and let them out in the morning to protect them unless your fencing is really safe. Ducks need a ramp to get into the house if it is not on the floor. They cannot scramble into nest boxes so as long as there is plenty of clean bedding, usually straw, they will make a nest.

Khaki Campbells are well known for their prolific laying with some strains reaching 300 plus eggs a year.

Ducks are waterfowl first and foremost and need water. They must have at least a small, moveable pond such as a child's rigid paddling pool, but larger ponds are much appreciated.

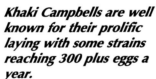

Ducks are not so fastidious about laying in a nest so you will see eggs in the pen and around the area. Collect eggs twice daily.

Foxes and other predators

Foxes love chickens but they seem to be even more attracted to ducks. Good fencing and housing will stop attacks but in some areas free range is very difficult as foxes come in daytime. Rats are also attracted to ducks, they love duck eggs and will take ducklings which is why scrupulous cleanliness is essential. Watch out too for winged predators - hawks, crows and magpies. Smaller ducks such as Calls are vulnerable and you may need to provide a mesh roof to your run. Ducks are frightened of dogs so the family dog can be the worst predator – keep them away from your poultry.

Sexing ducks

As ducks grow up, they make different sounds. A duck makes a definite 'quack' while a drake makes a sort of a croaky whistle. The other telltale sign is that drakes have curly feathers in the tail. Although drakes are not noisy you must not under any circumstances, keep

Ducks need to preen to activate their preen gland which makes their feathers waterproof and keeps them healthy. To do this they need to be able to submerge themselves in water and at least a small pond must be provided.

Some duck breeds are prolific layers. It is important to collect them twice daily if necessary so that they don't get dirty.

more than one drake to small number of ducks. They have a voracious sexual appetite and will injure and even kill ducks with their relentless treading. It's fine to keep drakes without a duck, they seem to be quite happy and don't fight and ducks will lay happily without a drake.

Duck ailments

Ducks are hardy creatures if kept correctly and although there are a number of complaints they do get, few are normally seen. Common problems are:

Worms – these come as roundworms, gizzard worms and gape worms and a large infestation of any of them causes damage to the bird's system, resulting in weight loss and lethargy. They can easily be prevented by using a wormer and your vet or agricultural merchant can advise.

External parasites can be a problem for ducks but are less so. Take all the usual precautions, thoroughly clean the house, use louse powder as directed and make sure broody ducks are free of parasites when sitting. Leeches or ticks need to be removed and the source identified. Watch out for maggots which can affect heavy-feathered birds around the vent.

Lameness is the biggest problem for ducks with their webs being easily damaged by stepping on something sharp. The injury which may have originally been slight, shows itself as bumble foot where there is a swelling. Broken and strained legs are usually the result of having an over-active drake continually mating with the duck or having too many drakes.

Breathing problems will be avoided largely if the house is airy and dry and you don't feed mouldy food. Any other causes must be treated immediately by a vet as it will be an infection and could even be a serious ailment like avian flu which is notifiable to the authorities.

Crop binding is when the crop becomes impacted and will need prompt treatment from a vet. Eye problems are nearly always due to insufficient water but if this is not the case it is likely to be an infection and must be treated by the vet.

Always seek veterinary treatment in the case of a health problem. Isolate the bird and keep it warm and dry, providing food and water.

It's important to only have one drake to a number of ducks as too many drakes will injure the ducks, even causing death. Ducks can live without drakes and drakes can also live as bachelors.

Ducks for a small garden

There are certain breeds of ducks that can adapt quite happily in small numbers to a smaller garden but they will still need access to some water.

Checklist

All new poultry keepers should make sure that
- There is nothing in your deeds or planning that prohibits the keeping of poultry.
- Consider your neighbours – are they likely to object and how can you persuade them that poultry won't be a nuisance?
- Cleanliness. All poultry needs to be kept clean but in an urban setting, it must be scrupulously clean.

Also remember

- The need to provide a small pond that the ducks can get in and out of such as a rigid-sided paddling pool with a ramp
- Hard standing but not sharp stones round the pond or keep moving it.

- Keep water and young children apart.
- Smaller breeds of ducks are usually the ones that can fly rather well!
- Foxes visit small gardens even in towns.

The breeds most suitable for small gardens come under the heading of bantams, miniature (small examples of the larger breeds) and the characterful Call Duck.

The Call Duck, as its name suggests, is very noisy. With the ducks weighing around 0.5 kg (1 lb), they open their little bills and let fly with a loud and continuous quack. Therefore they are not ideal for close neighbours. But they are a really appealing duck with large eyes and shaped like a 'rubber duck', round-bodied with a generous head and small bill. They come in an ever increasing range of colours with white being the most traditional through to the modern 'chocolate orange'. They have close family ties and a trio will stick together (two ducks and a drake). As they are so small, not only do foxes find them attractive but so do many other predators

A white Call duck enjoys a moveable small pool which can be easily emptied and cleaned on a daily basis if necessary. Make sure the ducks are able to get in and out easily.

including hawks. They are vulnerable to domestic animals such as dogs and the ducklings are so diminutive that they need considerable protection. It's best to net the top of the pen – which will also stop them flying away.

As they are small and light, they don't make a lot of mess and can manage with a very small pond or large washing-up bowl. They are not good egg layers but they are excellent "guard ducks" – you'll always know if someone is about by their loud quacking. They are easy to tame, naturally friendly and busy all day long!

The Silver Appleyard Miniature is a distinct breed from the Silver Bantam duck which is lower in numbers. It is small version of the famous Silver Appleyard duck from the 1930s and was introduced in the 1980s. These are very attractive in colouring and a most ornamental duck but also a useful layer of 100 or so eggs a season. They also make excellent mothers and it's hard to stop them going broody.

The Crested Miniature is a relatively new breed too, only accepted as a breed standard in Britain in 1997. They have become quite popular though stock may be a bit difficult to source. As their name suggests, on the head is a crest which should show as an even circled "pom-pom". It sits on the head, not over the eyes. But these are incredibly difficult to breed to get this characteristic and the best examples tend to be kept for exhibition. For the garden, a slightly less perfect example would still be attractive and ornamental and a bit easier to find. When they mate, the drake tends to hang on to the crest which damages it and also ducklings will not all be crested. Not a bird for the amateur breeder but great for the garden as it enjoys foraging and is a good egg layer at up to 100 eggs. It is acceptable in all colours.

Call ducks are so attractive that it is easy to add to the collection. These ducks have plenty of space but it's best to keep lower numbers in a smaller area.

Ducks for a medium garden

More space means more choice

There are even more lovely breeds of ducks that can be kept in a medium to large garden.

Checklist

- The larger and heavier the duck, the more mess they will make. Never be tempted to overstock.
- If you let them out to free range don't feed your ducks on your patio or at the back door and don't let anyone else do this. Ducks are very intelligent and will take camp there with the resultant mess, waiting for handouts!
- Think about providing a permanent pond but it must be one that you can clean and should have slabs round the outside for easy cleaning. Some water plants withstand ducks better than others.
- Ducks will be of enormous help if you let them out into the garden to forage. They seek out slugs and

snails and other garden pests and will help keep the numbers down. Some commercial horticulture and vineyards keep Runner ducks especially for this. But beware, a duck cannot tell a prized plant from a weed so if using this method of pest control, keep ducks away from any plant you particularly value.

The Indian Runner duck is always a talking point when seen for the first time. It is as though a duck has been stood up and elongated and is very unusual when seen for the first time. They look lean and active and they are, becoming more active when worried and the runner part of the name is also true – these ducks can get up quite some speed and cannot be accused of waddling! It has a serious side as its genetics have been

The Indian Runner is a striking duck with an upright carriage that is exaggerated if the duck is alarmed. They do not fly but are very active and can run very fast.

used in all the well-known laying breeds of duck such as the Khaki Campbell. In the past laying achievements of up to 300 eggs were recorded but now it is between 150-200 eggs – still a fantastic average for an elegant but also amusing duck. It's the duck of choice for gardening help as it is quite light and doesn't do as much damage as heavier breeds while being outstanding for foraging. It's not a good broody, though some ducks do manage to raise a few ducklings. It doesn't fly and it isn't that keen on water though as with all ducks it needs access to splashing water and does appreciate a small pond. The males are very active sexually so only keep one per several females, who get easily injured with their attentions. It's fine to keep males only as they rarely fight and live together

The Khaki Campbell is a larger duck, and can do damage with its feet in the garden. Because of this they require more space and be careful not to overstock.

quite contentedly. Some sheepdog demonstrations are sheepducks instead and the Runner is usually the choice for this as they flock well. Just be sure when you get your Runners that they are confined for a week or so as they can take off at high speed if they are nervous. Similarly, be careful with dogs or small children chasing them. They come in an ever increasing range of colours including White, Chocolate, Blue, Fawn, Mallard and Trout. The Mallard colour is just that, and is quite surprising to see – a wild Mallard marked duck

Indian Runners together with the crested Bali duck look very impressive as a flock and are sometimes used to replace sheep in sheep dog demonstrations as they can be driven.

It is advisable to keep ducks and chickens apart, especially in the housing but sometimes they do choose to mix. The group of little Call Ducks are keeping themselves separate!

that is upright! The Bali duck is similar to a Runner in shape but has a crest on its head.

Three light breeds that were developed in the 1900s for egg laying, have placid temperaments and will do well in a reasonable sized area are the famous Khaki Campbell, its derivative the Welsh Harlequin and the Orpington. The Campbell is khaki coloured as its name suggests (so named as Britain in 1901 was involved in the Boer War). It loves to look for slugs, snails and insects and doesn't fly. It's quite a robust and active breed so can make a mess, so don't overstock, but with

an egg layer supremo that lays over 250 eggs a year, you won't need to. As with hens, because of its high production of eggs, it needs good quality, balanced feed to do this. Not a good mother, unlike the Welsh Harlequin which is a very hardy duck and lays around 150 eggs. This is also placid and doesn't fly well. The Orpington was bred by the man who developed the Orpington chicken and is a good garden bird, doesn't fly well and lays up to 200 eggs a year. Of the three it perhaps needs more swimming water than the others and is a good mother.

Ducks for a large garden

Water, water everywhere...... Perhaps you have a natural stream or pond in your paddock, or want to put in a good sized area of water yourself. With more space and more water you can look at the giants of the duck world, the heavy breeds.

Checklist

- The heavy breeds are just that so do you have enough room to keep them in a reasonably clean environment?
- What sort of water do you have? If it is a stream be careful it does not run too fast and sweep your ducks away. If it is a pond, be careful that the ducks don't foul it – again, restrict the numbers.

- If providing a pond for the bigger breeds, you will need a bigger pond and as they are less active it needs to be easy for them to enter.
- The breeds that do well in a large garden will do very well in a more extensive area too but the smaller breeds will need some extra protection from predators.
- Watch out for foxes – larger ducks are easily taken by a hungry fox.

The Aylesbury duck is the archetypal large, white duck seen in smallholdings and ponds all over Britain. Or is it? Buying a true Aylesbury is quite difficult to do and the true Aylesbury is considered rare in all countries. The duck that is often referred to as an Aylesbury is at best a part-bred or more usually a

The pure bred Aylesbury is a rare breed. It is often confused with the commercial white duck. True Aylesburys have a pink bill and are big ducks.

commercial type of duck that is raised in large flocks for meat in the supermarkets. It's still a lovely duck, lays quite well and is good for meat although they sometimes get too heavy for their legs, but if encouraged to forage and fed a balanced ration, the weight can be controlled. They will have tell-tale orange bills. The true Aylesbury has a pink (flesh coloured) or pale pink bill and strong legs supporting the deep body. It will also have blue eyes. To obtain this bird you will have to go to a specialist waterfowl breeder who is aiming at exhibition quality.

The history of the Aylesbury is fascinating and the raising of these meat producing ducks dominated the small country town. Before the advent of the train the 'duckers' walked their ducks the 40 miles or so from Aylesbury to London and had to protect their webs by covering them in tar and sawdust. Conditions in some of the cottages rearing these ducklings were indescribably unsanitary and new demands for cleanliness in water and sewage put paid to much of this duck industry in the late 1800s. It remains an important part of poultry heritage. It's a placid breed which loves to eat and shouldn't be allowed to get too fat. It's really too heavy to fly and must be encouraged to range. The duck can weigh up to 5 kg. Eggs vary between 35–90 or so.

The Cayuga (and the bantam breed the East Indian) are known for their wonderful black plumage which should carry a beetle green sheen. The Cayuga is

Although often called Aylesburys, white ducks with orange bills are usually some kind of commercial or crossbred farmyard duck. They often lay very well and are still a delight to keep.

placid and hardy and fattens well but produces dark meat which is not to everyone's taste. It really needs plenty of water to maintain the marvellous green lustre and black plumage. It's a good average layer at up to 100 eggs and interestingly the first eggs have a sooty exterior with white eggs underlying.

The Rouen and the Rouen Claire are two separate breeds with the latter being lighter and a touch more upright than the Rouen but they do look similar and are both very large, placid, non-flyers. The Rouen duck weighs around 4.5 kg and the Rouen Clair is a little lighter. As with the Aylesbury, they need to be encouraged to exercise by ranging or foraging as they can get far too fat which is bad for their legs. Both lay around 100 eggs but were really kept for their meat. Now they are kept for their beauty and for exhibition as their striking Mallard markings and size make them breathtaking.

The Silver Appleyard is an all-purpose duck developed for eggs and meat and is also a good mother. The attractive colouring which is a mixture of silver, claret and green for the drake and silver and a flecked brown grey for the duck is another advantage. Developed by the famous breeder Reginald Appleyard in the 1940s, it lays from 100–200 large white eggs a year and also has a lovely temperament. The miniature

The Cayuga duck needs plenty of water to get the best from it's lustrous plumage - black with a beetle green sheen.

The Rouen Claire is a very placid, heavy breed of duck that needs to be able to forage to keep them from getting too fat.

An attractive Rouen drake showing off his striking white neck collar and green sheen on his head. Note the curly tail feathers that indicate he is male.

The Silver Appleyard was bred by the famous breeder Reginald Appleyard in the 1940s to be a utility (eggs and meat) breed. Nowadays, many people keep it purely for its beauty.

was developed in the 1980s by respected waterfowl breeder Tom Bartlett and is equally gorgeous.

The Muscovy duck is the only domestic duck not originally descended from the wild Mallard. It originates from a perching duck from South America and some people feel it is more goose-like though it is definitely a duck. They are different to the other breeds and a bit 'love them or hate them'. They don't behave in the same way, preferring to perch and they are excellent flyers despite their weight of around 3 kg for a duck and up to over 6 kg for a drake. They are impressive in flight, less so if they are yours and making a bid for freedom! Some people record their Muscovies as flying off for the day and returning at night which is perhaps acceptable if you have a village pond, less so if your rather startled neighbour suddenly finds his Koi Carp pond full of splashing Muscovies.

The Muscovy does not originate from the Mallard like all other domestic ducks but from a perching duck. They can fly well and hiss when alarmed with their head crest raised.

Having said that, they are not over keen on water although as with all ducks they need to be able to splash and preen, but they are keen on foraging, even eating small mammals if they can find them. In appearance many people think they are ugly with their red skin on their face and 'caruncles'. The crest on their head can be raised or lowered, often with accompanying hissing. The colour most commonly seen is the mainly Black but now there are Blue, Chocolate and even Lavender. They are good natural mothers and lay reasonably well. All other ducks have to incubate their eggs for 28 days – for the Muscovy, a very different duck, it is 35 days.

The dabble of tiny feet

Ducks, like hens, rear their young by sitting on eggs and hatching them. They will then take care of the young, keeping them warm and encouraging them to feed and eat until they can manage on their own.

If you want to rear ducklings the natural way, first make sure that your chosen breed has a good reputation for rearing its own young. Some breeds really don't sit or make very good mothers. For these you will need an incubator or an obliging bantam hen. Hens can hatch out duck eggs very successfully though get a bit surprised when their brood takes to the water later on in life (young ducklings reared by hens are not waterproof – don't let them go near water or they will drown).

A broody duck behaves in quite an agitated, almost distracted way. She makes a distinct nest which she lines with her own feathers. If she does this in an insecure place where a predator can take her or her ducklings, you will either need to move it (not usually

Young ducklings require a dry bed, a warm pen and heat if they are raised away from a duck. Drinking water should be provided but they should not be able to immerse themselves.

A bantam hen will sit the extra seven days (duck eggs take 28 days to hatch) to rear ducklings. Don't let them near water until they are several weeks old.

A group of Muscovy ducklings. Vulnerable at an early age, you should keep an eye on them so that there is no chance of them encountering predators. Muscovy ducklings take longer than the normal ducklings to hatch.

very successful) or build protection around her (usually the better idea) and provide her with food and water. She will make a hissing sound that you will not have heard before when you approach her and ruffle up her feathers, looking as fierce as she can. She'll lay a clutch of eggs and then start sitting when she considers she has sufficient. The advantage is that she will control the turning and humidity of the eggs and knows exactly how to get the best hatch; the disadvantage is that she may well lose interest half-way through, be satisfied when she has hatched a duckling or two and leave the rest of the eggs before they hatch or even crush some of the eggs or ducklings. You can only protect her and let her try. If she repeatedly disappoints, don't let her go broody again but take her eggs away and use a broody

hen or incubator. Consider too if you could have made the hatch more successful – perhaps she was bothered by external parasites or felt threatened by other ducks or domestic animals such as dogs.

After 28 days (35 for a Muscovy) the ducklings will hatch and you must keep them safe and secure and away from the other birds and possible predators. Provide preferably duck crumbs for the ducklings but chick crumbs if that is not possible, feed for the duck and drinking water for duck and ducklings. At this stage don't provide swimming water – young ducklings can get chilled and drown. If reared by a broody don't provide swimming water for at least a month until their own preen glands work. If the duck abandons the ducklings or even turns on them, you need to provide heat for them, so use a dull heat lamp and in absolute emergencies, a radiator or other heat source – but be careful not to cook them! Ducklings are as messy as ducks and create havoc in nice clean pens so be prepared to freshen the pen often.

Geese in your garder

Geese are grazers and they need a good sized garden or orchard to do well. Pic 3 Why geese? Because they are intelligent birds that are a pleasure to watch or because they are excellent as guards, letting people know when there is someone about. Some breeds are moderately good egg layers of up to 60 or so eggs a year and if you can bear it, nearly all breeds are good for the table! Geese can live to be very old with 30-year-old plus geese not unusual, so they are a long-term commitment.

What do they need?

Geese do not like too much confinement and need a good sized area in which to roam and graze. Commercially, it is not possible to 'battery' rear geese as they require grass and therefore they are raised in large flocks on a grass area with a safe barn for night time.

As with all poultry they need to be protected from the fox – their size does not mean that they can defend themselves from this predator.

Ideally a goose will have clean, well grown (up to about 10 cm is good) grass to graze all year round but in reality the winter tends to make most areas very muddy and in summer, unless you have an extensive area, it quickly becomes overgrazed. Do not keep too many geese on an area to avoid these problems and if possible, move them on to fresh grazing to allow the old pasture to grow. The rule of thumb is no more than five geese per acre and less is better. They will need fencing in – or neighbourhood dogs and children need fencing out.

The house can be a simple large garden shed but must be strong to keep out predators such as foxes, badgers or loose dogs and have good ventilation. It must be dry as well. As with all poultry, if the outside enclosure is not fox-proof – and as you will need quite a decent area for your geese to range this will be difficult – then they will need shutting in at dusk and letting out in the morning. Each goose requires about one square metre of space within the house. If it is too hot, wet or small, then respiratory problems will surely follow. Shelter too needs to be provided outside if it is very open. Orchards are good because trees give shelter.

Pasture for geese needs to be checked for poisonous plants such as deadly nightshade, yew and of course, commonly seen in gardens, laburnum. Also check for dangerous and sharp objects. Grass reaches its highest food value in late spring and although it has good value throughout the summer, it does decline in the autumn

African geese, like Chinese geese, originate from the wild Swan goose and have a distinctive knob at the top of the bill as shown by this one who is enjoying the summer grass.

White Chinese geese grazing on a good height of grass. Being very vocal, Chinese geese make particularly good guard geese but might be too noisy for close neighbours!

A flock of white geese look impressive in the sunshine but they do consume quite large quantities of grass. Good fencing keeps these geese inside the paddock and helps to keep dogs out.

and is nutritionally poor in the winter. Therefore supplementary feeding will be needed at these times.

As with all young creatures, geese grow the most quickly in their first months of life. They need balanced and adequate food during this time to lay down foundations for their future life. This is the time to feed crumbs as dry mash might cause them to choke. From 6-8 weeks feed growers pellets and then from four months onwards adult rations if there is not sufficient grass to keep them nutritionally supplied. Young goslings are very vulnerable to ground predators, dogs and winged predators such as raptors so keep them well protected and when you first let them out on to fresh grass at a few weeks old, make sure they are kept safe.

All geese need grit to enable their gizzard to function properly; this is the bird's answer to teeth and it breaks down the fibrous material. Place grit in a container where the geese can access it easily.

As with all waterfowl geese need not only continually accessible drinking water but also they need water for splashing. They must be able to totally immerse their head and necks and need enough water to be able to vigorously splash to keep their feathers clean. Ideally they should have a larger 'pond' either as a large moveable tray or round container that is deep enough for them to swim in or you might like to

A gander becomes very aggressive in the breeding season towards any intrusion including his owners. He has one mission and that is to protect his mate at all times.

Wild geese such as the Canada goose, move from area to area in search of good, fresh grazing and are very successful breeders when they have safety and good nutrition.

construct a pond. All ponds will need washing out so construct them with this in mind. If using water that is naturally available on your land, make sure it is safe, that it doesn't run so fast that the geese get washed away, or too stagnant.

Geese need worming and the two most commonly seen are gizzard worm and gape worm. Contact your vet for worming advice but it is a straightforward process.

Buying your geese

The usual way is to buy a pair or a trio. Unlike ducks and chickens, geese do mate for life and are devoted to each other. You need to be sure that your pair or trio are unrelated and are not siblings. Try to buy calm geese who are already reasonably tame – at the least don't run in terror when they see a human.

If you buy goslings, then you will need to provide a higher level of care as very young goslings need a lot of skill to rear. Warmth, protection, correct feed and protected water are the watchwords. It is quite possible to keep only females but not a good idea to keep more males than females.

Are geese aggressive?

They do have a reputation for fierceness but the majority of geese if correctly kept, are calm. But there are times to watch out for. A male (gander) will protect his mate and dogs should be kept well away from them as should any child who tries to chase them.

At breeding time, the gander becomes more defensive and if the goose is sitting on eggs, he will protect her to the best of his abilities.

A prize-winning example of the African breed. It is a very large and heavy breed. Although fairly hardy, frostbite can be a problem in cold weather, affecting the knob on the bill.

Which breed of goose?

Most goose breeds are descended from the wild Greylag goose with the exception of two, the Chinese and the African goose. These are thought to have the wild Swan goose as their ancestor and do show different characteristics to other breeds. Different regions developed their own individual type of geese, suitable for their particular needs whether that be a large carcase, a good mothering ability or sheer hardiness. There are even some breeds such as the Steinbacher that was developed as a goose for fighting! In the past geese were also valued for their feathers which were needed for filling mattresses, pillows and

Known as a 'Kampfganse', that is 'fighting goose', which can be seen by the short strong bill, useful for defending itself. Known to be aggressive but generally when provoked.

The Chinese goose showing off the knob. For egg laying, the Chinese goose is the choice and can produce in excess of 60 eggs a season. They have smaller feet which do less damage to sward.

quilts while quills were needed for pens. Abbeys and monasteries kept geese in flocks both for this and for goose fat.

Towards the end of the nineteenth century and with another big revival in the 1980s, the goose became an exhibition bird and now can be seen at poultry shows throughout the world.

Guard Geese

Most geese make good guard geese but by far the noisiest and most inquisitive is the Chinese goose. Pic.8 This is an elegant looking bird which has a knob at the top of the bill, causing it initially to be known as the 'knobbed or Asiatic goose' (together with the much larger African). Often seen with brown colouring, it can also be predominantly grey and also pure white. It is known for its loud voice so may not be ideal if you have close neighbours but because it is a light breed with smaller feet, it can be less messy than other breeds. They are not always ideal with small children as they can be a bit flighty. They are excellent egg layers though and can produce in excess of 60 eggs a season.

The Roman goose carries the distinction of having raised the alarm thus saving ancient Rome from a Gallic invasion. It also was likely to have crossed the Alps by foot.

It's one of the smallest breeds but is a meaty bird that lays moderately well – around 40 eggs a season. It is always white and may or may not feature a tuft on its head.

Auto-sexing

An auto-sexing breed is where you can tell the difference in the sexes by the colour of the plumage. In the case of the Pilgrim the ganders are snow white and the goose is a soft shade of grey with characteristic white spectacles. As geese can be very hard to sex, there is an obvious advantage in immediately knowing which is which especially when purchasing initially! They are a hardy goose that enjoys ranging. .

West of England is another auto-sexing breed with a pure white gander and the goose being grey and white. They are also very hardy and good grazers and usually have a calm disposition.

The Brecon Buff is a particularly hardy goose with very tight feathering, allowing it to thrive in harsh weather providing it has plenty of free ranging good grazing.

A champion Roman goose showing their well balanced shape. They can also be crested, which has been described as a tiny helmet perched on the top of the head.

Hardy types

The Brecon Buff is known for its hardy character and they are usually good parents. As their name suggests, they come from the hill farms of Wales where they were expected to live off grass and convert it to meat for the Christmas period. They do need a good area in which to range.

Big boys and girls

Geese breeds are divided into light, medium and heavy and it is in this latter category that the large farmyard geese can be found. Perhaps the best known is the Embden goose which originated in Germany. It is pure

The Toulouse is a magnificent, large goose, very stately in carriage, that does need very careful management and is not really a beginner's bird.

The well-known Emden goose which is a heavy breed. It is often confused with any white goose, many of whom are actually commercial hybrids.

white with blue eyes and an orange beak. They reach weights of up to 15 kg for ganders and nearly 13 kg for geese which makes them very large indeed.

The Toulouse is the goose with the very large dewlap and is a very stately bird, developed mainly for its ability to get a fat liver for pâté de foie gras production. Luckily now many people value them for their looks and for exhibition and they come in grey, buff and pure white. Good handling when young is important.

Because they are not keen foragers, they don't need too much room but because they have such large feet, it must be the sort of land that does not easily become muddy. They have lovely soft feathering but it does attract flies which to lay their eggs on them, especially near the vent, so fly strike (maggots) must be watched for. Not really a beginner's bird but very rewarding for those who are able to devote great management skills to their welfare.

The African is also descended from the wild Swan goose as is the Chinese but this is a truly large bird that weighs up to 13 kg for a gander and nearly 11 kg for a goose. It too has a knob on the front of the skull and, like its smaller counterpart, is quite vociferous.

Commercial Breeds

There are several commercial breeds of geese which are good layers of around 40 eggs or more and have lovely personalities. They are usually white which means small commercial geese can be mistaken for Romans, medium-sized for Pilgrim or West of England ganders and large ones for Embdens. Be careful that you are sure that you are buying a pure breed if that is what you want. If you do find yourself the owner of a commercial breed they are still delightful to be with and have been bred to be good egg layers to produce more breeding stock and good for the table with an efficient food to weight ratio.

To sum up

- Choose a hardy, straightforward breed to begin
- Make sure that if you want a pure breed that it is not actually a commercial breed or cross-bred
- Buy from the breeder if possible and see other stock
- Be clear if you want an exhibition standard bird – they will be a lot more expensive
- Heavy geese are very attractive but need well drained land and more attention – not best for beginners
- The Asiatic geese can be very noisy – think of the neighbours
- Visit a poultry show to see the breeds for yourself and talk to the exhibitors before making a decision.
- When you get your birds home, keep them confined in a smaller area to begin with while you get to know each other. Increase the area as they become more at home. Keep children and dogs away from the birds and work quietly and speak calmly around them.

The next generation of geese....

The gander naturally takes an active part in the rearing of the goslings and makes a proud and sometimes dangerously protective father. Make sure you protect the family from predators.

Breeding geese can be done in one of three ways, either naturally by the parents, by a broody hen, or by putting eggs in an incubator.

Most geese are good parents and both take an active part in the raising of the goslings. But Chinese geese can be rather flighty and heavy breeds such as Toulouse, Embdens and Africans can accidentally tread on their young and therefore kill a surprisingly high number. These may be better bred using a different method. For natural brooding, the watchword is 'supportive'. Interfere as little as possible; your job is to keep them safe from foxes and other predators and ensure they have sufficient water and food. Therefore you will need to either move them to a safe place or make the place they are in safe – sometimes they just will not be moved! Very young goslings are vulnerable not only to predators but also to getting lost in long grass, getting soaked in water (drinkers for the first couple of weeks need to be designed so that goslings cannot immerse themselves accidentally) and they can also find themselves on the wrong side of a fence to the distress and danger of themselves and alarm of their parents. A good airy building is the ideal situation initially, with access to fresh grass as the goslings grow but you might have to devise some fencing around where the goose has chosen to sit! If you can't guarantee the safety of the goose, then she cannot be allowed to brood. It is natural for the gander to stand protectively over her and when they hatch, the goslings, and for him to become more aggressive than usual. Keep calm and keep children, dogs and other domestic pets away from them.

Broody hens will foster goose eggs with great success. Be sure she can cover the eggs – a bantam can handle about three goose eggs comfortably. Ensure she is free of red mites and other parasites before she begins sitting.

Artificial rearing in incubators

A goose egg takes from 30–35 days depending on the breed whilst a hen's egg takes 21 days to hatch. Having hatched the goslings they will need warmth in the first three to six weeks of their life, depending on time of year.

A brooder will provide this and it can be as simple as a heat lamp suspended over an enclosure with solid walls to keep out draughts but high enough to stop escape. Bulbs are raised or lowered according to whether the goslings are huddled under it (too cold) or spread out away from it (too hot) but should never be closer to the floor than 50 cm. Provide gosling crumbs as feed and ensure they cannot get into the water and chill.

Depending again on the weather, they can go outside in a safe run with a shelter at a few weeks old but if it is cold or wet they must be brought in. Give splashing water after the first month and ensure they can easily get out of the water or they could drown.

Keeping geese healthy

If you keep your geese clean, well fed and not overstocked, with plenty of grazing, you should not have too many problems. These are the main things to look out for.

A healthy goose will be alert, bright eyed, feed well and splash and preen in the water.

If you have a sick goose they will be dull, perhaps have a discharge from their nostrils, lame, be messy round the vent, or losing feathers. Whatever the problem he or she needs to be removed and penned in a dry, clean enclosure. Lameness is a problem with waterfowl who have webs that can be easily injured on sharp stones, thorns or rubbish.

Discharge from the eyes is usually due to an imbalanced diet or insufficient clean washing water. Check that the diet is balanced, provide washing water and contact your vet for eye drops or ointment.

Digestive problems such as diarrhoea may be due to bacterial infection (perhaps due to unclean living conditions), worms, or, in young birds, Coccidiosis.

This gander is the picture of health. He is alert, with bright, clean eyes and no discharge from his bill and his feathers are clean and in good order.

Young goslings should not be given deep water while they are still in 'down' but they do enjoy splashing especially in warm weather. Make sure they don't get soaked and chilled if it turns cold.

All will need veterinary treatment with an antibiotic or wormer and neglecting this will mean that the rest of the flock will also be affected. Birds do die, especially young ones, quite quickly from digestive problems so act quickly to contain it, treat it and if necessary contact the vet for treatment.

Worms are primarily gizzard worm and gape worm. These are easily prevented by regular worming as indicated by your vet and by not overstocking and also by keeping water clean and having clean bedding.

External parasites such as mites, lice or fleas don't seem to trouble geese as much as hens but if you do see a goose constantly scratching or with feathers missing (apart from during the moult) then treat them with an anti-parasitic powder.

Geese can also suffer from frost bite in extreme weather, especially the knobs on the Asiatic geese, and from overheating in hot weather.

Talking turkey

It is easier to keep turkeys than many people believe but they do need some space and appropriate care. These large birds would not be suitable for a very small back garden. However, an area around 10 x 4 metres would be ideal for a trio – that is a male (tom) and two females (hens).

Housing is very important for this provides a safe place to sleep at night away from predators, protection from bad weather and a place in which to lay eggs. A secure shed approximately 2.5 metres x 2 metres, with ventilation, a perch pole about 0.75 metres high, shavings or similar litter on the floor will be ideal for a trio of turkeys that are outside during the day. This size of building would not be adequate for continual housing.

Turkeys will realise where home is and where they are fed and sleep but they will explore if there is no fencing. The clipping of one wing – two thirds up the primary feathers – will unbalance the bird and make flying difficult.

In late winter the turkeys begin to mate and if mixed varieties are together this will ruin any chances of them breeding pure in the coming season. It only takes one successful mating for a female to be fertilised for many weeks. About 28 days after mating eggs will appear and the female continues to lay throughout the spring and

A Champion Bronze stag turkey. Males puff up their feathers and display their tail in a fan to impress female turkeys. This is not aggressive behaviour.

An alert Pied (Crollwitzer) stag turkey. This is a European ornamental turkey suited for exhibition and egg production. It is called a Royal Palm in the USA.

A Slate stag turkey growing a new tail as he comes out of the moult. Slate and Blue turkeys were extremely popular at the turn of the 20th century.

summer but fertility lowers as the season progresses. Adult females running with males should wear a breeding saddle to protect them from damage caused by the male during mating. Saddles are made of pieces of thick canvas or leather, with loops of material at one end through which the female turkey's wings pass.

Turkeys will not thrive unless they are fed adequately, so turkey starter crumbs are given to day-old poults (baby turkeys). To entice poults to start eating chop up a hard-boiled egg very finely and mix with the crumbs. A chick drinker is suitable for small poults. Dip their beak into the water just once and this will show them where to drink.

Turkey grower pellets are fed from five to six weeks until about four months old when the birds are then transferred to either turkey breeding pellets, if they are to live, or turkey finisher pellets if they are for the table. Fresh, clean water daily is essential.

From six weeks onwards turkeys will require worming. Roundworms are the most common but the heterakis worm, which is a nematode parasite, is the most dangerous. This causes blackhead, a disease that attacks the liver and is usually fatal. Your vet will give advice on wormers that are licensed for or can be used on turkeys.

Good ventilation – but not draughts – is vital in turkey housing. Turkeys suffer from respiratory problems without it. They can also pick up problems through being on damp or dusty litter. Mycoplasmas can cause sinusitis in turkeys, where the sinuses in the face are swollen through mucous building up. This should not be ignored as the bird may eventually suffocate.

Although a large bird it does have predators - foxes, raccoons and mink are all life threatening. Crows will steal eggs and rodents spread disease, so a vermin control programme may be necessary. If in any doubt get a professional pest control officer to deal with the problem.

If you understand how to properly look after turkeys they will give you immense joy and if keeping a couple as pets you will certainly enjoy their company.

Norfolk Black hen. Typical example of the variety which is very placid and ideal for exhibition as well as meat production.

Keeping quail in the garden

This diminutive bird can produce large numbers of decorative and edible eggs. Quail were once wild in Britain and are a member of the pheasant family. Because they are very small, they can be kept in small areas but they have to be fully confined as they are excellent flyers and are not likely to stay around if let loose. They are ground dwellers and traditionally used to live in aviaries to clear up dropped seed. There are several different types but it is usually the Japanese and Italian Coturnix quail that are kept for meat and egg laying. There is a larger type as well known as the Bobwhite that is not such a good egg layer but is sometimes kept for meat. The Chinese Painted quail (Excalfactoria chinensis) is about 4–5 inches in height, much smaller than other members of the quail family such as Japanese and Harlequin quail.

There are several types of quail but the Coturnix quail is usually the one that is kept for egg laying.

Specialist quail feed will keep them healthy and mealworms and millet fed loose encourage them to scratch in the shavings.

Most people keep quail for their attractive eggs which are still regarded as a delicacy and some take it a step further and keep them for meat. Japanese quail should lay up to 200 eggs which is a lot of eggs. They come into lay at around 50 days old. An increasing reason for having quail is because they are delightful, busy birds and are enchanting to watch.

Ideally the birds like to live in an aviary-type situation with a good-sized wire front to keep them interested in the outdoors. Shavings on the ground provide dust baths while boxes lined with hay inside the aviary provide places to shelter, hide and breed.

Quail eggs are very attractive and are seen as a delicacy although a bird may lay up to 200 eggs a year.

A large cage gives them room to move and even to stretch their wings. Fine mesh is required to stop them escaping and boards to protect against small predators.

Quail do not have a good reputation for being very good parents so hatching in an incubator is the usual method of breeding them.

Large cages with feed and water will provide protection for the birds though it is nice to provide features for them to jump on or hide behind, thus giving them interest.

Some people keep them in large rabbit hutches and some in poultry arks. A rabbit hutch-type arrangement or small cage is rather boring for the birds but might be necessary for winter accommodation. The advantage of the arks is that they can be moved around so that the birds have a new area to search for snippets of food, keeping them busy and interested. If very wet then move them onto hard, dry ground or even bring the ark into a building. They will need protection from cold winter weather. Because they are naturally ground dwellers you cannot expect them to walk up a ramp to a higher house from their run – they want ground-floor accommodation. It is important to ensure that the area is rat free as a large rat can easily take a quail and probably would find it quite easy to penetrate most cages. Get rid of rodents the moment you see any signs of them.

They are small birds so they don't require huge amounts of food, about 150 g per bird per week, and it is now possible to buy specialist quail food fed from a small poultry feeder. They also love mealworms and millet and if you spread them on the floor it keeps them busy scratching for them. If not on grass, try growing pots of grass to put in the enclosure or tear up tufts of grass from the garden for them to peck at. As with all poultry, provide pots of grit. You might have to crush it into smaller pieces. Clean water is important; quail don't like to drink stale water. They do not have a reputation as "tidy" layers, laying eggs more or less where they are, but some strains will use shallow plates lined with straw for nests so it's worth a try!

Domestic quail are not good breeders and usually their eggs are put into incubators. Quail can fly soon after hatching so any brooder must have a mesh roof and they are amazingly small when they hatch. Perhaps an easier method is to rear them under a small broody bantam. A quail will live for up to two years.

They are entertaining to watch and although they make a pleasant chatty noise, they are not loud. Be sure to site their housing where you can watch them!

Quail need clean bedding and feeders to keep the feed fresh. They tend to lay rather randomly although shallow plates lined with soft straw might encourage a nest.

Eggs and incubation

Incubators come in all sizes from 6 eggs to 6,000 plus so there is bound to be one on the market to suit your needs. It's great fun hatching eggs and very educational.

Although artificial incubation has been practised successfully since ancient times, it is a skill that needs to be mastered and some say it is an art as outside factors influence the hatch. For many, a broody hen is a preferred "incubator" as artificial incubation is only as good as the person operating the machine, the eggs you put in and how the instructions are followed!

Before you hatch any eggs ask yourself what you are going to do with the adult birds and if you are able to cull the surplus cockerels; it's not the answer to keep them or send them to market – even quality pure breeds have more cockerels than hens and they have to be removed. It's easy for even experienced breeders to get carried away with hatching and overstock.

So what is an incubator? It is a machine that keeps eggs at a temperature that allows the embryo inside to develop and hatch.

A basic incubator for up to 12 eggs is relatively inexpensive and is all you may require.

Forced or still air?

An incubator can be still air or forced air. Most these days are forced air and this is where a fan circulates the warm air equally over all the levels of chicks. The correct temperature for inside an egg is 38°C (100°F) and to achieve this a forced air incubator needs to run at 38°C and a still air at 39.7-40°C. Carefully check the instructions for each machine.

Manual or automatic?

The other choice is whether you turn the eggs or if the incubator turns them. This is called manual or automatic. A hen is constantly turning her eggs to prevent the embryo sticking to the shell and to distribute the nutrients within the egg. Eggs in an incubator need to be turned at least three times a day in opposite directions. Up to seven times is better but for most people, three times is a big commitment and works very well. Obvious disadvantages are that it gets forgotten and some members of the family may turn them too vigorously. Big advantage is that it can involve all the family and make them feel a real part of the hatching process and you can have a chart to record the temperature every time you turn them which will really help you to know you are on the right track. But most incubators now are self-turning and the advantage is that they do this in a slow, even way and several times a day. There is no chance of forgetting to turn the eggs. You need to stop turning about three days before the eggs are due to hatch.

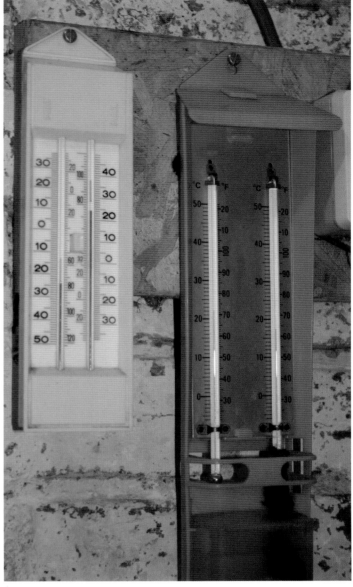

Chicks hatching in a semi-commercial hatcher for larger numbers of eggs. Smaller machines often incorporate a hatcher for up to twenty or so chicks.

Temperature and humidity are of vital importance in artificial incubation. Easy to read and accurate thermometers are essential.

What is a hatcher?

When buying an incubator you should ask if it has an in-built hatcher. Ideally you want a machine that has both. Following the manufacturer's instructions, it is normal to change the trays within the machine to convert to a safe place for the eggs to hatch on the due date. Then you will need to have a brooder handy, either a purpose-built machine which is useful if you are doing a lot of chick rearing, or more usually, a heat lamp suspended over a safe enclosure.

If you buy a second-hand incubator you must be sure that it is free from disease so you will need to thoroughly disinfect it, using a type of liquid recommended for this process. You will also need to disinfect your own incubator after every hatch.

Where to put the incubator?

It needs to be sited in a place with a constant temperature, not near draughts or open doors. Eggs are affected by a change in temperature and swings in weather, such as a heavy frost during the hatching period, can and do cause losses. Alternatively, over heating such as in a heat wave, is equally problematic.

It has to be on a level surface and it needs to be safe, where it can't be knocked over or bumped into and also where people don't keep opening the lid to look at the eggs!

Humidity

Humidity plays a big part in a successful hatch. A hen will naturally control the humidity of the eggs but most incubators will require water added at a certain point in the cycle. Much has been written on this subject but the golden rule is, follow the manufacturer's instructions and keep an eye on the weather outside.

Candling

This is where light is shone through the hatching eggs to check the progress of the embryo inside. It is a skill that really needs practice but firstly get a chart of how the egg should look through the hatching period. What you are looking for is an embryo and the size of the air

sac. At the end of the hatching period, the air sac will be about a third of the egg. Too small and there is too much moisture in the air, too large and there is not enough. Both will result in the egg not being able to hatch. Initially, don't worry too much about this, just watch for the dark shape of the embryo and for an increasing air sac. A "clear" egg is one where no embryo has developed; it is not fertile and should be removed before it goes bad and affects the developing

An egg candler that will take all types of egg makes for an accurate assessment but a simple strong torch will do initially.

A commercial incubation room which is free of draughts and unaffected by sudden changes in temperature. Charts record the progress of the hatch.

eggs. Don't candle the eggs until at least five days in the incubator and then only do it once a week, keeping the time that the incubator is open to a minimum.

Record keeping

A simple chart recording the daily temperature of the machine and the temperature in the room, the weather and the results of candling will help you understand what went right and what went wrong with every hatch.

A smaller incubator which is hatching quails eggs. The chicks from these are very small and nimble!

Hatching

Hatching takes place over some hours and is initiated by "pipping" when the hatchling starts to break through the shell. You must not help the hatchlings; if you intervene, it is quite possible that they will be unable to develop and you will have to cull the chick. Leave them in the hatcher for 24 hours before transferring to your ready brooder. Chicks are wet to begin with and need to dry. Leave the unhatched eggs for a few days but then candle and discard if dead. Dead in shell is remarkably common and usually due to the incorrect development of the air sac so that the occupant simply cannot break out of the egg. That's why you need good records to try and reduce this happening in the future. It is distressing to see a fully grown chick dead inside the egg but sadly it is also not uncommon. The best thing to do is to be sure to learn for the next hatch.

Finally, the initial selection of eggs will play a big part in successful hatching. Only use clean, well-shaped eggs and discard any cracked, thin-shelled and oversized or undersized eggs. Store point down in a cool but not cold room (definitely not the fridge) and bring them into room temperature before placing in the incubator. Do not place eggs in at different times but keep the eggs and then place them in the incubator in one batch. They should not be more than a week old before placing in an incubator.

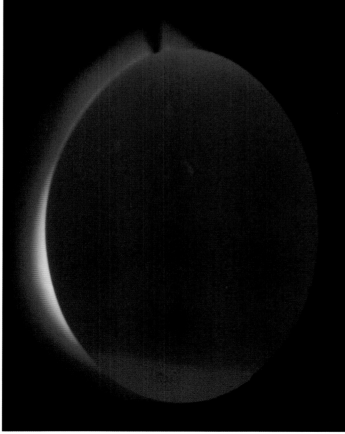

Looking into an egg when it is on the candle, showing that the egg is fertilised.

A simple but effective brooder with heat lamp and draught proof sides. There is space for the chicks to get away from the direct heat. Inner corner blocks stop chicks getting trapped.

Happy hatching

- Read the manufacturer's instructions
- Get a chart of how an egg should develop
- Keep good records
- Site the incubator in a room with an even temperature and no draughts
- Disinfect the incubator before use
- Choose sound eggs

Incubation periods

Hens – *21 days*
Ducks – *28 days except Muscovy ducks, 35 days*
Turkeys – *28 days*
Quail, Japanese – *16 days*
Quail, Bobwhite – *23 days*
Geese – *30 days, light breeds up to 35 days, heavy breeds*

Eggs for all reasons

An egg is a highly nutritious, delicious food which these days is readily available and often undervalued. Fresh eggs have a flavour all their own and the delight of collecting a still warm egg from a nest never wears off. The colour of the shell does not influence their nutritional value at all and although the UK prefers brown eggs, some other countries believe white eggs look "fresher"! Now we also have a choice of various shades of brown, green and blue eggs – if we are prepared to pay for them or keep the appropriate breed of chicken. Duck, goose and turkey eggs are also edible and have slightly different but attractive flavours in their own right and quail eggs, as well as being good to eat, provide a decorative addition to a dinner table.

So what is an egg?

It has five basic parts, the yolk of course, the egg white (albumen) and the shell are obvious. Less obvious is the germinal disc inside the yolk and the shell membrane, inside the shell. There is also a small air pocket which increases if the embryo is to hatch. To check for freshness you can put them in cold water. Those that stay at the bottom horizontally are fresh. If they lean to one side they are less fresh, if they sit vertically in the water they should be cracked and used perhaps in baking, but if they come up to the top then they have gone bad.

Fresh eggs at a market always have a huge appeal. Duck eggs are particularly good for baking due to their higher fat content.

This is because the air pocket increases as the egg ages due to the porous nature of an egg shell.

The question is often asked, can I eat fertile eggs? That is, any egg where a cockerel is kept and the answer is yes. The only proviso is that you need to stay on top of collecting them and any that are found under a broody hen should either be discarded or left to hatch. Collect them twice a day if possible.

Do I need a cockerel?

Poultry will lay eggs without male birds and you can keep a flock of laying hens without a cockerel; in fact, the high egg laying breeds are bred not to go broody.

How nutritious is nutritious?

Very! A hen's egg is about 70 per cent water, 11 per cent protein and 10 per cent fat. The fat is largely unsaturated. They are a very high source of protein and also contain all the vitamins except C. An egg, depending on size, is between 70-80 calories – it's the mayonnaise and frying fat that increase the calories, not the product! Duck eggs are a little richer and contain more fat than hen's eggs, which make them particularly good for baking. They are also larger. Turkey and goose eggs can be eaten boiled by someone with a good appetite but are more usually sliced and shared or used as a single egg omelette or quiche!

If storing in a fridge then keep in egg boxes so they don't absorb smells of any other foods and take them out of the fridge for a couple of hours before using. If you have a cool pantry, then this is the best place to keep eggs. The pointed end should be downwards and keep them apart from strong-smelling foods. Keep them separate in egg boxes; if you have a bowl of eggs

Although selling eggs to friends and neighbours usually comes without regulations, sometimes egg stamping is a legal requirement. Hand held stampers are relatively inexpensive.

If selling at markets or shops there are clear guidelines to the legal requirements for the labelling. Egg boxes can be bought to your individual need.

Pickling your surplus eggs from the summer to eat during the cold winter days is a real treat!

and one is bad it will penetrate the shells of all the others.

Most poultry keepers find they have eggs all year round. There will be fewer in the winter and when the poultry are moulting but in the spring and early summer there is likely to be a surplus. Eggs can be stored in various ways. Waterglass (soluble sodium silicate) was a favourite method years ago – it is very important if you use this method that none of the eggs are cracked or washed as the solution seals the pores of the shell. Freezing is an option but they must be frozen without their shells and they must be fresh. Freeze whole eggs in small quantities. Some people like to freeze the whites when the recipe calls for yolks only – they can be used in meringues later. Pickling is another option and can be great with cold meat after winter roasts.

Selling eggs

In most countries, you can sell eggs direct from your garden to friends and neighbours if you don't grade them and you have a small flock. Once you take them to market then various regulations such as egg stamping and grading may be necessary although these are rarely prohibitive. Although eggs have had a bad press with Salmonella, especially duck eggs, it has been shown that it is rarely the raw egg that carries this but more often a cooked egg contaminated by someone who is carrying the bacteria. But to be absolutely sure it is advisable to thoroughly cook eggs, especially for vulnerable people or pregnant women. Cleanliness in producing the eggs is also essential as is regular collection. It's best not to wash eggs and this can only be achieved by keeping nest boxes very clean and also the area around the house – muddy runs mean muddy feet mean dirty eggs! If you have to wash, remember egg shells are porous so use water slightly warmer than the eggs to close up the pores and wipe clean with paper. You can buy egg washing machines but management should be the first priority. Ideally, keep washed eggs back for baking and sell your clean eggs.

Collecting, using and eating your own fresh eggs is a satisfying experience. You'll soon be searching out egg recipes too!

Showing your poultry

Poultry for exhibition have been popular since the mid-nineteenth century when the Victorians discovered the fun of taking their birds to a show. There are poultry shows held all over the country, sometimes as part of a bigger agricultural show and sometimes put on by poultry clubs. All types of domestic poultry can be shown and as well as a huge range of classes for chickens, there are also classes for domestic ducks and geese and for turkeys. Most shows are for pure breeds only but a few smallholder club shows sometimes have classes for laying hens or best presented poultry. Poultry show exhibitors are often known as "fanciers" and the poultry show men and women describe themselves as being "in the fancy". It's a very inclusive hobby with people of all ages and from all walks of life and in comparison with some other hobbies, relatively inexpensive. The largest outlay should be on buying show-quality stock direct from respected breeders and housing and feeding it correctly. The entry fees for shows are reasonably modest with the cost of getting there as an additional expense.

In Britain, the Poultry Club of Great Britain governs the shows and the breed standards (what the perfect example of each breed should be). They have well over 120 poultry clubs affiliated to them plus the individual

A prizewinning Blue Laced Wyandotte bantam showing off her correct plumage. A winning bird can go home with some impressive cups.

To get the feathers on a big Black Orpington large fowl as clean and distinctive as this takes a considerable degree of skill.

On a Black mottled Barbu d'Uccle Belgian, it is important that the leg feathers are clean and unbroken and that the muff and beard are clearly visible.

breed clubs. A big Championship show is held in late winter. In the USA there are the American Poultry Association and the American Bantam Association. It is a popular hobby throughout the world, from Europe to Australia and also in Asia.

Visit a show

To find out what goes on, first visit a show. There is quite a choice of shows, from Poultry Club Regional Championship status to very small local club get-togethers but they all share a passion for poultry and exhibitors are very happy to answer questions. The birds will be in uniform wire cages with no identification as to who owns them. They will normally be penned by around 9 am and then judging commences. The judge has a steward to write down the results and they both wear white coats. By early afternoon the judging is completed and the public and competitors are allowed back into the hall where rosettes and certificates will indicate the result. There is often a catalogue so you can see who owns which bird. It's worth taking time to study the winners as they will be good examples of their breed type. Most shows have a "Championship Row" where the winners of each section proudly pose. These will be such categories as Best True Bantam, Best Soft Feather, Best Hard Feather, Best Waterfowl and so on, including Best Eggs.

Egg showing is also a skilful pursuit with colour, size and uniformity closely considered. There are often separate classes for children which may involve showing how they handle their birds. Some shows have decorated eggs and photographs as well.

By mid afternoon the judges will have conferred to choose their Best in Show and Best Opposite Sex in Show or Reserve Best in Show and prizes will be presented. Birds are "boxed up" around 4 pm for winter shows and a bit later in the summer and exhibitors go on their way with their awards. Results

Prizewinning White crested black Poland shown to her best advantage - she has been trained to stand alertly and to be unafraid of humans.

Bathing is an essential part of preparing for the show. If you bird is well handled it should not be too alarmed by what is, for the bird, a frightening experience.

and perhaps a critique can be read in the poultry press afterwards. Sometimes there is a sale section at the show which is separate to the competitive section where breeders bring their stock and it's often a good place to buy some quality birds.

Starting showing

It's quite easy to start poultry showing. First of all, try to join a local poultry club so you can start at evening meetings or members-only shows to get some experience. If this isn't possible, choose your local show and carefully study the schedule. Entries normally have to be in a few weeks before the show so decide what you are going to take and then there is time to get it ready.

The bird should be at least average for the breed standard and not display any major faults. There is no point in taking a bird that has the wrong markings, the wrong shaped comb or no bearding when it should have some. Be objective when you look at the bird and use the Standards Book to make your decision. Next, the bird needs to be reasonably tame. Ideally it should be "pen trained", that is, used to being in an

exhibition cage and to being handled. Some fanciers train their birds to stand outside the pen for judging and photos. You won't get disqualified if your bird is not tame but it is better for the judges and far better for the bird if it is at least used to being handled. Homebred chicks that are intended for the show pen can be acclimatised to handling at a very early age.

The bird needs to be clean. You will get disqualified if there is any sign of mite or scaly leg as these are contagious. The day before the show it will need washing and again, the tamer it is, the less stress this will be for it, and drying. In the winter, washing a bird and putting it outside in the cold will cause illness and even death so it needs to be dry and kept inside after its bath. Transport to the show must be strong, safe and have enough room for the bird not to be cramped. It needs to be clean and have some flooring such as newspaper covered with clean shavings. Be vigilant about ventilation – in the winter the birds still need air and vehicles or trailers can get too hot if there are a number of birds. But you do want to avoid direct draughts. In the summer, it is important to guard against overheating. There are regulations relating to

transporting poultry and it is important to ensure you adhere to them.

On arrival at the show, collect the pen numbers and put the bird into the pen. Be very careful as you handle it not to damage feathers. Food and water should be removed for judging so it is best to get there early so you can offer your bird some food and a little water prior to this. Most shows supply containers but bring white clip-on containers just in case they don't and you will need to supply your own food. A show kit too is handy, some water and shampoo for last-minute stains, some baby oil for combs and wattles, some old toothbrushes for cleaning feet and legs, towels and kitchen paper. When the judges enter the hall, competitors have to leave – normally heading for the excellent breakfasts provided at most shows! In the afternoon, see where the bird has been placed and take the time to ask why it won or why it didn't as time spent with experts is never wasted.

But beware, showing is an addictive hobby that can gain many friends and even take you all over the world!

A Yellow Dutch male presented immaculately. The legs are spotless and the comb is clean and without any injury. Every feather is in the correct place.

Pigs in the backyard

The cottager's pig, kept in a stone sty near to the house eating scraps from the kitchen, was a common sight up until the 1950s. Now it is more difficult to keep pigs this way. Feeding waste to pigs is strictly controlled and meat is never allowed, and neighbours usually prohibit the keeping of a pig close by. But if you have a good sized garden, with a large airy stone building or room for a modern pig ark and no near neighbours, then pig keeping might be for you.

Why keep pigs?

Pigs can provide bacon and pork for your freezer but also pigs can be pets and provide companionship. Pigs can help gardening by providing manure to compost for vegetable gardens and they are delighted to help you turn over rough ground. Pigs, if well kept, are clean and straightforward to look after. But there is no doubt that pigs have a pungent smell, even if kept very clean, so you need to be prepared for this.

On a small amount of land there are two main options for pig keeping: to keep a weaner to pork or bacon weight (depending on the breed around six months or more) or purely as pets. Choice of breed is important as commercial pigs get absolutely huge so the garden pig needs to be from a relatively small breed such as the Berkshire or the traditional cottager's pig, the Gloucester Old Spot. Another possibility is the Oxford Sandy and Black. The Berkshire is a black pig and is made more attractive by having white feet and a white tip to its tale. It is hardy and thrifty. The Gloucester Old Spot has a fatter carcase than the Berkshire and does

Piglets are very appealing but they do need very good fencing as they root under fencing as well as pushing against it. They can clear land for future vegetable growing for you!

well in cold conditions. The Oxford Sandy and Black is a docile pig that thrives on rooting.

The Kune Kune has gained a reputation as an orchard pig as well as a back yard pig and can make a delightful pet but also is good to eat. The Kune Kune pig originates in New Zealand but it's a subject of some conjecture as to how they got there as it appears they are not indigenous to that country. But it is known they were kept by the Maoris for meat, living not in enclosures, but free to scavenge around the houses. This probably explains their love of humans and excellent temperament. Kune Kune pigs vary from 24 inches to 30 inches high and weigh between 140-220 lb. Kunes are steady in their characters, and are extremely easy to handle. They are very gentle, and ideally suit the new pig keeper who may be intimidated by larger, more boisterous pigs. Because of their small size they do not cut the land up as much as larger pigs.

On the pet side there are the Vietnamese Pot Bellied pigs who with their appealing wrinkled faces and intelligence become very much part of the family. Their meat is not usually to the UK taste, though valued in the Far East.

Whatever pig you choose you will need to sort out identification and movement and register with Defra before the pigs or piglets arrive. Pigs of any age moving from your holding to a market of any kind must be permanently identified with the Defra herd mark of

Pigs are naturally clean if given plenty of straw and not overcrowded. They do though have a 'piggy' smell which is not to everyone's taste!

The Gloucester Old Spot is a very traditional English breed that has been much loved by cottagers and smallholders through the years.

your holding. Any pigs aged one year and over that you move off your holding must be permanently identified with the Defra herd mark of your holding. All pigs moving to slaughter are still required to be permanently identified with your Defra herd mark and movements of pigs under one year of age between holdings can be identified with a temporary mark. These do change so check before taking delivery of your pigs.

Pigs of all sizes are immensely strong and housing needs to be able to stand up to digging, rooting, pushing and shoving. There are some excellent arks on the market but they will need a strong fence around them to contain pigs. You could convert a brick-built outbuilding but it needs to have good ventilation. Pigs do like to root so it is important to set aside an area for them to devastate. Of course, if you have an overgrown garden, then electric fencing around the area and putting pigs in will go a long way to solving digging problems and remove many of the weeds and slugs. Pigs need shelter in the hot sun and ideally a wallow. Provide plenty of straw for the bed and the pigs will be

The Vietnamese Pot Bellied pig is the ultimate pet pig and owners claim it is very intelligent and affectionate. They have the same basic needs as all pigs though and the same rules and regulations.

Oxford Sandy and Black pigs enjoying a wallow and rooting in the soil for grubs and roots. Pigs do get sunburnt and shade is necessary and a wallow much appreciated.

much cleaner though you will still need to muck them out regularly. A rubber water bucket clipped to the wall should solve the problem of having them use it as a football.

What goes into the trough?

Pigs have a reputation for living on waste products but to achieve health and meet modern requirements, they need to have a balanced diet. Pigs love to eat!

They love to root in their straw beds, in their pens, and if at pasture, in the grass and mud. Feeding time should also be fun for pigs and they need to be fed at least twice a day and to be able to look for food for at least part of the rest of the day. A foraging pig will find grass, grubs including earthworms, roots and fallen fruit to supplement its diet in a healthy way. So a confined pig also needs to be 'busy' – perhaps searching out waste vegetables and roots as well as the balanced ration that you will need to provide. Bagged pig feed is readily available and is designed for the purpose so you can buy feeds that range from piglet creep feed to pet pig feeds.

Meals must not be fed dry – pigs like wet feed and you can add surplus goat's milk to a feed in a trough.

Pig troughs are the usual way to feed and this way you can dampen the food. They need to be kept clean

Pig breeding is not for novices but when undertaken good facilities and experience will stand you in good stead. Pigs love a straw bed!

A ready made pig ark which with suitable fencing, would provide housing for a couple of garden piglets. Plenty of straw in the house will keep them clean and warm.

Pigs using a traditional feeder which allows more than one pig to eat without touching and is heavy so does not tip over. Pigs love to eat!

– if the pig soils them do not tip food on top. Make sure you provide enough trough space as there are always shy pigs that stand back from their more greedy mates and as a result they will lose weight and suffer stress. The other method is to throw the nuts over a wide area and leave the pigs to root for them which will keep them busy. Rolls or cakes are not fed in troughs but are ideal for outside pigs and are distributed over a wide range so that even the shyest pig gets sufficient food.

Ensure that you have vermin-proof storage for the bagged feeds. Not only is it costly to lose good food to vermin such as rats and mice but also they can transmit disease to you and your pigs and will need to be controlled. Don't encourage them in the first place by giving them free meals. Also excess food (uneaten wasted food) will certainly attract them. Adjust your rations accordingly (pigs tend to eat less in hot weather) and if a pig is not taking the food it should, then consult your veterinarian.

If your pigs have access to good grass, they can consume up to ten pounds or so a day but the grass would need to be readily accessible. Seven pounds of good grass could replace about a pound of pig feed.

Whatever the end objective for your pigs, keeping them on a small scale means you can get to know them and make their lives more pleasurable. Remember, they are big, strong animals with a nasty bite when roused so treat them with respect as, like all large animals, they can be dangerous. Keep a strong fence between the pigs and children or domestic pets to be on the safe side and learn pig handling skills before becoming a pig keeper.

The middle white is content being able to rootle in the ground. Middle whites achieved their most popularity between the wars as a specialist pork breed.

The British Saddleback pig was once popular as a cross to produce hardy, docile outdoor pigs but is now on the At Risk register of the Rare Breeds Survival Trust.

Goats in the garden

Goats played a big part in cottage life throughout history, showing themselves to be an important source of dairy products during both wars.

Goats were kept for their milk on market gardens up and down Britain prior to and during the Second World War. They were often tethered on verges during the day or let loose on common land and housed at night. William Cobbett in the 1820s, writing in his famous Cottage Economy, pondered: "Goats are pretty creatures, domestic as a dog, will stand and watch, as a dog does, for a crumb of bread, as you are eating; give you no trouble in the milking; and I cannot help being of opinion that it might be of great use to introduce them amongst our labourers".

How much space do goats need?

There is a system of goat keeping called zero-grazing whereby goats are kept housed, and branches, forage such as fresh-cut grass and hay are brought to the goats. But goats do like to be outside so you would need to have enough space for them to have a fenced area around their house or a separate enclosure with a shelter. They are browsers rather than grazers so they thrive on woody fibre which comes from tree bark, leaves and branches. If your enclosure has none of

Goats can jump and also get underneath quite small gaps so good fencing is needed to contain them. When they are horned, ensure they cannot get trapped in the fence.

Goats will graze grass which needs to be reasonably long and clean but they are known as browsers, eating more fibrous plants and trees in preference.

these things (or they are eaten), then you will need to cut branches for them to enjoy. Your enclosure should also feature a strong box or two for them to jump on and off. All goats require particularly effective fencing as they are great escapologists and always want to be the other side of where they actually are! They can squeeze through gaps, get down on their knees and wriggle under fences plus clamber or jump over fences. Therefore if goats are to be a permanent fixture, so must the fencing be, with close-set post and rail at a good height, perhaps lined with wire sheep netting (but not if your goats have horns). There are electric fence systems that also do the job but beware of them getting caught in it and being damaged or killed as a result if they cannot escape from the pulses. If the battery gets flat they will simply walk through it as they will constantly try it. If you have a good garden on the other side of the fence, you want to be sure the goats stay put. Tethering is the last resort and if done, needs a proper swivel collar and chain and constant vigilance to see they are not hanging themselves. They need water available all day – especially important if producing milk as this requires considerable intake of liquid, so make sure the container doesn't tip over.

The house needs to be draught-proof but airy and the same applies as with the fencing: it needs to be well built. A stable or other outside building can easily be adapted or use a well-built shed. Pens need to be at least 1.5 m by 2 m for a single milker or two goatlings. You can partition off a store (be really careful the goats cannot get at the feed) and also an area for the milking

Young goats are very playful and inquisitive as this young Nubian and Toggenburg show in their efforts to escape from their pen.

stand. Light will be needed. It's best if goats can look out of the building. The building needs to be on hard standing and have hard standing round the entrance Pic.11. Hayracks are best designed with a lid and put high enough so they cannot get in or on them. Goats climb when they can. Water buckets will need fixing with a ring or clip. Ensure that all bolts are goat-proof – they are very clever at escaping.

Goats are herd animals so two should always be kept. There is no need to keep an entire male and it would be a mistake in a garden situation as they are strong smelling with some unusual habits! A neutered male is acceptable and can be a lovely pet.

There are so many reasons for keeping goats. They are wonderful dairy animals and "run through", that is they can milk for a number of years after kidding without having to give birth every year to stimulate the milk supply. If choosing a dairy goat, then the standard of management will need to be even higher than usual with the commitment of milking twice daily and of having an understanding of udder care and an awareness of mastitis and other udder problems. The goats will need a balanced ration suitable for milkers for, in proportion to her size, a goat produces more milk than a cow. Unless you have a large family that requires a lot of milk, choose a dairy breed that doesn't swamp you but milks steadily such as a Golden Guernsey. This is a smaller goat that is an attractive golden colour giving milk that has a high butterfat. The high-yielding dairy breeds include the Saanen which gives around four litres of milk a day, a staggering amount in proportion to its size. White in colour, this goat is placid and has a long lactation even in the winter – possibly due to her Swiss ancestry. The Toggenburg is a smaller goat, again has a long lactation

and produces similar quantities of milk to the Saanen. The British Alpine is also a heavy milker but more active than the others, making it a little more difficult to manage.

Goats can also be kept as pets and as harness goats. There is a Goat Harness Club but a period when Blue Tongue disease was in the UK made it difficult for people to attend shows. Harness goats tend to be neutered males and they are trained for this task. They do not pull very heavy weights but are very striking to see.

The Pygmy goat is usually kept as a pet as it is a very small goat that originated from Africa. In stature they are cobby and compact but are very lively in character.

To horn or not to horn. People hold strong views on this but horned and non-horned goats should not be kept together and disbudding needs to be carried out before the horns grow as they have on this young Saanen.

The Golden Gurnsey provides a good but not excessive quantity of milk that has a higher butterfat and is a charming goat for beginners. It was once classifed as a Rare Breed.

All goats have to conform to current tagging and movement regulations as this young Toggenburg clearly shows. Keep up to date with current legislation and abide by it.

They are very intelligent and if kept correctly, are rarely ill. They are not usually milked due to their small size which makes milking difficult. They need the same care as any other goat.

Angoras and their crosses have a lustrous fleece which is used for spinning and is particularly popular with home spinners. Neutered males or females are equally suitable and these are known as fibre goats.

All goats have to conform to current legal requirements which do change, sometimes quite quickly, so it is best to contact Defra to get the up to date information. But the basic requirements that you must adhere to are that you have to have a holding number for your property before you bring any goats on to the land, even pets. Contact your local Defra office for details – this is free of charge. All goats must be identified with an ear tag or tattoo showing the herd number and an individual number. This is done by the breeder and you must check it has been done as it is illegal to move a goat without identification.

The dimunitive Pygmy goats make great pets and are usually kept for their lovely characters and amusing antics rather than for milking as their teats are very small.

You will also need a Movement Licence before transporting your goat and this is obtainable from your local Trading Standards Office.

Daily care

Goats will need a good supply of fibrous food such as hay but they also like lucerne haylage and, if you can find it, clean pea straw. They are bedded on fresh straw and need cleaning out regularly. The waste can be composted for the garden. Depending on their enclosure they may get some nutrition from browsing or grazing or from branches cut for them. Beware of poisonous plants, in particular laburnum, yew and rhododendron. In addition they need a balanced ration which can be bought ready mixed in a bag. There is a special Pygmy mix available as well as general goat mixes and dairy goat mix. Choose the one appropriate for your goat's needs. Although popular belief has it that goats can eat anything and everything, this is not true and to keep them healthy they need to have a correct diet. They will also need a mineral block – check it is suitable for goats as some are not.

Healthy goats

Hoof trimming is essential and they will need checking every two months. You can do this yourself after an experienced goat keeper has demonstrated. Regular worming is also a must as are vaccinations – check with your veterinary surgeon. Lice are more attracted to goats than other livestock so keep a look out for these and treat immediately if found. There's no reason why you can't groom your goat with a soft brush.

Goats are delightful, alert and inquisitive creatures that enjoy human company. Whichever type of goat you decide to keep, join a goat club and find out as much as you can before you start – and also meet like-minded people and their goats!

The Swiss breeds such as the Toggenburg provide very large quantities of milk as they have been selectively bred for many years.

The cuddly looking Angora goat is a great source of top quality fibre which is in demand from home spinners - or you could learn to spin it yourself! It is not milked but is a good mother.

Young goatlings enjoy the clean bedding in their water and draft proof house. These are all without horns and so the risk of injuries is reduced.

Starting with sheep

Sheep require constant supplies of fresh grass and quickly graze a small area. However, a large garden could support a couple of hand-reared orphan lambs with supplementary feeding.

Even large gardens are not the place to keep sheep permanently but if you have a large area of grass and plenty of time, rearing a couple of orphan lambs could be a rewarding experience. Restricted areas of grass won't keep them going for more than a couple of months so the plan would be to move them to more suitable pasture later on in the year or feed additional food to bring them to a suitable weight for your freezer. But it's handy if you are bottle feeding to have them close to the house although the downside is that you won't be able to emerge from your back door without being loudly noticed!

You will need a large area of grass and some suitable fencing. You could use hurdles and keep moving them to fresh grass or you could invest in some electric fencing. Sheep are great escapers so it needs to be well maintained. A shelter is very important and it needs to be dry, warm and have clean straw bedding. Clean water that cannot be tipped over and a mineral lick complete the essentials.

Plenty of time is needed to successfully rear orphan lambs and to begin with you will need some help from an experienced shepherd. Commercial sheep farmers

To keep breeding sheep you will need a large paddock and a good knowledge of pregnancy, lambing and lamb rearing plus some indoor penning.

New born lambs in a well strawed and secure pen. They usually remain in with their mothers for a few days. Three lambs may require extra bottle feeding.

The Leicester Longwool are known for their good fleeces which are particularly in demand by hand spinners. It's a good idea to go and look at sheep breeds at a show or exhibition.

often have orphans for sale at a low price as they are quite a commitment to rear if the premises are not geared up for it. Ensure that they have received their colostrum – that's the first milk produced by the ewe and contains the protective antibodies they will need to thrive. Check too that they have been tagged or that arrangements are made for it to be done. When beginning with sheep, always buy lambs that have been feeding from a bottle for several days and are doing well. As you get more experienced, then younger lambs will be a possibility. Organise yourself with milk powder, bottles and lamb teats and get some good quality hay. Initially, the lambs will be contained in the shelter with a good straw bed and clean water, fed by you with a bottle. They need to be fed every few hours,

It helps if you can teach your lamb to lead with a halter, not only if you want to show but also just for moving. Tamer sheep are easier for the small flock owner.

As sheep get older their teeth change. A yearling has two permanent incisors while a four year old has eight, making it a "full mouth". After this they may well lose teeth and older sheep can be "broken mouthed" (few or no teeth).

even through the night to start with, and the equipment needs to be thoroughly cleaned between each feed. Full instructions for mixing the feed and what quantities are needed for what age will be on the milk replacer itself. Offer hay from a week or so old and on dry, warm days, let them on to the grass. The aim is to get them to eat roughage as early as possible as hand-reared lambs tend to get "pot bellied" in appearance. Expect their droppings to be firm but yellowy; if loose or runny then the milk could be incorrectly mixed or the bottles or teats were not properly cleaned. Any problem with lambs must be dealt with immediately by consulting the vet as lambs go downhill very quickly. Once you have got them to a few weeks old they can be out all the time with shelter available and they will normally be fine. Follow the instructions for bottle feeding and over the next few months increase the roughage (grass if sufficient but otherwise hay) and give some sheep pellets and gradually reduce the bottle feeds. They can eat some garden vegetables but not potatoes or tomatoes. If they do find their way into your garden, they will decimate it.

The lambs will be very tame. Do bear in mind that they will turn into large, strong sheep and don't start any practices you can't sustain. For example, bringing month-old lambs into the kitchen for their bottle might be cute but you haven't really any room to complain if fully fleeced sheep then try and do this for the rest of their life!

As with all livestock, sheep need to be kept clean and mucked out on a daily basis with the waste composted somewhere away from the house and neighbours. Lambs will need vaccinating against the major sheep diseases including blue tongue and will also need worming – consult with your vet. As they grow they will need spraying with a special insecticide to prevent fly strike where flies lay eggs on the fleece and maggots bury into the flesh or anus of the lamb causing pain and death. It is a good idea to "crutch out" when the fleece grows, that is, to remove the often dirty

Jacob sheep can have two horns as in this picture or four horns. Horned sheep can and do get caught in sheep netting but are not usually too agressive except for rams and mothers with lambs.

A sheep fully and humanely restrained. Traditionally they are shorn on their backs but this can be less stressful for sheep and owner.

wool around the tail and anus area of the lamb to help discourage flies. Their hooves will also need regular trimming. If you haven't already, you will have to register with Defra and follow their regulations regarding sheep. You cannot move your sheep without observing the current rules so you need to ensure that you are familiar with them as you will want to move your now young sheep to new pastures. Find out exactly what breed your orphan lambs are – they may well be a selected cross-breed.

There are many breeds of sheep, usually specific to an area. The mountain and hill breeds (upland) tend to be smaller and more agile (and wilder!) while the lowland breeds grow bigger and are more placid. Among the most well known of the upland breeds is the Welsh Mountain, which is bred to survive without much human intervention in severe conditions. The fleece is excellent as a knitting yarn. The Badger Mountain is white with black eyestripes, hence their name, but they can also be the reverse, black with white eye stripes. Hand spinners like the naturally coloured wool. The Swaledale originates from the

Different coloured Shetland fleeces don't have any value in the commercial world but they are of interest to hand spinners and it's sometimes possible to get premium prices for good fleeces of different colours.

Sheep must be sheared every year to protect them from flystrike and becoming too hot. Cleaner sheep make for better fleeces.

The Portland is a small but hardy sheep that are often foxy-red when born but change to white as they get older.

The distinctively marked Kerry Hill is a hornless sheep that originated in Montgomeryshire. It is an outstanding mother and is known for its hardiness and longevity.

highland of North Yorkshire and is very hardy with a fleece suitable for carpets or tweeds. Among the lowlands, most people will have heard of the Suffolk which grows to a large commercially meaty carcase that is known for early maturity. Placid in temperament, it may require more intervention in lambing than the hardy upland breeds. The Oxford Down and the South Down (of which there is a miniature variety), look like teddy bears with a leg at each corner, the Oxford having a black face. Both breeds are renowned for their placidness and early books talk about them being ideal for "the lady shepherdess"!

Primitive breeds such as the Soay and the Hebridean date back into early history and are not really suitable

A moveable sheepfeeder which not only keeps the hay dry but also prevents it from blowing round the paddock. It is large enough to allow the flock to feed together.

for back yards. The Hebridean and the Manx Loghtan are multi-horned and can grow up to six horns. They are remarkably hardy but do need space. Jacob sheep are distinctively black and white horned sheep which many keep for home spinning their fleece but also because they are lovely to look at as well as useful! Some sheep such as the Herdwick produce coarse wool for carpet making while others like the Shetland sheep have lustrous fleeces for fine knitting. It's quite possible to home spin your sheep's fleeces and black or brown sheep make especially attractive naturally coloured knitwear. Very few sheep are now kept for their wool as commercially it has a very low value, in some years costing more to shear than the money received, so it is meat that is the predominant reason for commercial sheep farms. There is a small but increasing number of sheep being kept for milk production – these are the specialist breeds of British Milksheep and British Friesland. For those not wanting

to worry about having to shear sheep there is the Wiltshire Horn, which is a large white faced breed that is a woolless breed. It's a kindly sheep which makes them suited to lowland situations and is a good doer. As sheep must be shorn every year sometime from May onwards, this can be a great saving in labour if you don't want any wool.

You might want to show your lambs or sheep at your local agricultural or smallholding show and there are usually classes for every breed and type. You will need movement licences to travel to a show and to adhere to animal transport regulations so check with Defra before entering. Sheep must be bathed before the show – choose a warm day and plenty of time to dry. Some

shows judge the sheep in the pens but many expect you to lead your sheep around the ring so halter training prior to the show is an essential. The earlier you start the better, as soon as they are weaned or in the case of orphan lambs, as soon as they are a few weeks old. Use sheep nuts or treats to entice them and be very patient. It's a good idea to train backyard sheep to lead anyway. Also teach sheep (this one is not hard!) to follow a bucket – it makes them much easier to catch when you need to handle them. The more you get to know your sheep, the pleasanter it will be to keep them so time spent with them is never wasted!

The Southdown is a placid sheep that is quick to put on weight from good quality grass. It is a good beginner's breed.

There are many colour variations in the Shetland which is a small but determined sheep with a good fleece for homespinners. Note the ear tag - it is a legal requirement that all sheep are tagged.

Beekeeping in gardens and cities

Keeping bees has long been part of the "market garden" scene. Given certain precautions, honey bees can be kept anywhere, from the corner of a field to the suburban garden or flat roof in a city. In a field, the hives should be fenced against livestock, if applicable. In a garden, care must be taken to avoid causing problems for neighbours. On a roof, hives should be protected against the wind. Beekeeping is particularly suitable for those with only a small area of land, requiring somewhere to stand the hives with adequate space for the beekeeper to work during his/her colony inspections. The apiary (where the hives are kept) should be large enough to accommodate spare hives which may house a swarm temporarily or hold part of a colony during swarm control manipulations.

Unlike bumblebees or solitary bees which have an annual life cycle, the honey bee colony persists from year to year. It will occupy any suitable cavity, from a hollow tree to a cavity wall to a beehive. It consists of

Worker honey bees are female and perform a number of tasks within the hive before becoming foragers.

The male drone is only present in the hive during the active season. He can be identified by his large eyes, broad thorax and rectangular abdomen.

The queen is larger than the workers with longer legs and a longer, pointed abdomen. She is the only one that lays eggs and is the mother of all the bees in the colony. Marking her makes her easier to find.

Multicoloured pollen stored in the comb indicates that it has been gathered from a number of different flowers.

One of the tasks for the worker honey bee is to guard the entrance.

Beekeeping in gardens and cities

workers, drones and a single queen. Normally only the queen lays eggs and she is the mother of all the bees in the colony. The workers are sterile females. They secrete beeswax with which they make comb consisting of hexagonal cells which are used for rearing young (the brood) and for storage of honey and pollen. They perform different jobs according to age – house cleaning, feeding larvae, guarding and foraging. Male drones are designed to mate with virgin queens, usually produced during swarming. Drones are produced each spring and ejected from the hive in autumn because they are no longer useful.

Honey bees visit flowers to collect nectar which they convert into honey. Nectar is carried to the colony in the honey crop and honey stored for use during the winter when it is too cold for bees to fly from the hive and few flowers are in bloom. The crop is also used to collect water. When foraging on flowers, pollen sticks to the bees' hairy bodies. They use stiff hairs on their

Pollen is brought back to the hive packed in the worker honey bee's pollen baskets.

A worker honey bee forages for nectar on blackberry.

back and middle pairs of legs to bring this together and pack it into pollen baskets on their hind legs. In the hive, pollen is stored around the brood nest and used in the production of "brood food" for the developing larvae. Bees also visit flowers specifically to collect pollen. Foragers recruit others in the hive by indicating the distance and direction of the nectar/pollen source with a figure-of-eight dance. The number of times the bee "waggles" her abdomen while running up the middle indicates distance. The direction indicates that of the source, relative to the sun. Bees collect propolis, the sticky secretion of some tree buds, use it to draught-proof the hive and varnish over any debris too large to remove.

Worker honey bees forage for nectar and pick up pollen on their hairy bodies. This is packed in the pollen baskets and taken back to the hive.

Foragers recruit other bees by performing the 'waggle' dance which indicates the distance and direction they have to fly to find the source of nectar or pollen.

The sticky tree resin, propolis, is carried back to the hive in the pollen baskets and used to fill cracks and crevices.

A new beekeeper is strongly recommended to start with at least two and probably no more than about six colonies. A small number, especially if these are nuclei which are about half the size of a full colony, gives a chance to gain experience as the colonies progress. With only one colony, it is impossible to know whether it is doing well or badly. A second colony provides a comparison and can also be the source of very young larvae from which the first can raise a replacement queen should its own get lost.

Beekeepers are duty bound, particularly in urban areas, to keep docile bees which are not quick to sting and colonies which do not swarm readily. The bees should not cause problems or anxiety to neighbours. Facing the hive entrance near to a high hedge or fence makes bees fly up when leaving the hive and they are then less likely to cause problems to neighbours. Bees should be trained to a water source near the apiary and this must never be allowed to dry out. This will minimise problems with bees drinking from next door's pond. These factors must be considered when choosing an apiary site, particularly in built-up areas.

Bees can be purchased as a nucleus or full colony.

The nucleus colony which fits into a half-size box is a good way for a beginner to start.

Worker honey bees sting to defend their nest. The barbed sting cannot be withdrawn and is pulled out as the bee flies away.

The vendor should give a minimum guarantee that there is a queen, a certain number of frames of brood and food, and bees. They should say when the colony was treated against Varroa and with what. There are four notifiable bee diseases in the UK – American Foul Brood (also notifiable in the USA), European Foul Brood, Small Hive Beetle and the mite, Tropilaelaps. The last two have not yet been found in the UK. The beginner should learn the appearance of healthy brood and get help if anything looks wrong.

A new beekeeper is advised to attend an introductory course, read at least one good book,

The beekeeper needs to know what a healthy brood looks like with dry, slightly domed brood cell cappings and pearly white larvae lying in the shape of a 'C'.

subscribe to a beekeeping magazine, especially one with advice for beginners, and join the local beekeeping association. These will all prove invaluable particularly throughout the active season.

Choice of hive is personal but it is worth considering the most popular one in the area. Second-hand equipment will be more readily available but should be checked for soundness and absence of disease in bees and combs.

The minimum personal protection should be a veil. Other protective clothing includes overalls, gloves and rubber boots. Worker bees sting to defend their colony. Stings are painful and can lead to an allergic reaction – in extreme cases, anaphylactic shock which can be fatal. Generally, a beekeeper becomes immune to stings. Anyone put off by the thought of being stung

The smoker and a hive tool are essential for easy colony manipulations.

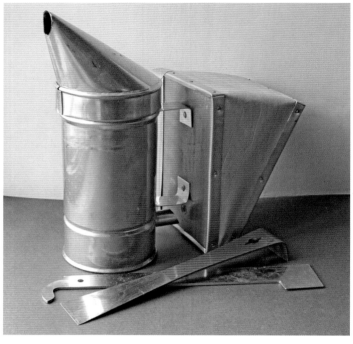

should think hard about beekeeping. It is not a hobby for everyone and deserves to be enjoyed. A hive tool and smoker are essential. There are two types of hive tool, both with positive qualities. Smoker fuel should give a cool smoke. Hive records are essential for noting colony development, swarm control, beekeeper manipulations, honey crop, etc.

Colony inspections should start in spring when the weather warms up. Swarming preparations begin when the queen lays eggs in queen cells, built on the face of the comb. If the queen leaves with a swarm, virgin queens will emerge and take out further swarms or casts until one mates on the wing and returns to head the colony. Swarm control is extremely important. It prevents bees causing a nuisance and keeps the colony together for a maximum honey crop.

As the colony develops, additional honey storage boxes or supers are added. When these are filled, they are removed from the hive and the honey extracted. Colonies must be treated against the Varroa mite, generally in autumn. Colonies must be fed to ensure they have sufficient food for winter. Winter gives the beekeeper time to review and plan for the coming

Swarming can be considered to be colony reproduction. Steps should be taken to control it and ensure that it does not cause anxiety to neighbours.

A veil is the absolute minimum protective clothing required. Veils are available in different patterns.

The swarming colony will raise new virgin queens in queen cells especially constructed on the face of the comb.

As the season progresses, additional boxes called supers are added to the hive to give the bees additional room for honey storage.

season, mend equipment, buy additional items and learn by reading and attending lectures.

As well as the pleasure and fascination of looking after bees, beekeepers can also enjoy the products of the hive. Honey is a delicious food. It can be sold but must be extracted, bottled and labelled according to the appropriate legislation. Beeswax harvested during honey extraction can be used for candles, polish, cosmetics and soap. Propolis and royal jelly can also be collected but this is not cost effective on a small scale.

Honey is a delicious food.

Colonies need to be fed for the winter to ensure they have sufficient stores. The first feed is given in the evening when bees have stopped flying to discourage robbing.

Going Large

After successfully keeping poultry and livestock in your garden, where can you go next? The next step might be to rent or buy a small paddock and that opens more doors to bigger livestock such as alpacas, llamas, small ponies, miniature horses and donkeys.

Alpacas and llamas

Llamas, guanacos, alpacas and viçunas, the South American camelids, originate on the high altiplano in Peru, Chile and Bolivia. Only the llama and alpaca have been domesticated and they are now kept around the world. The llama, used as a pack animal, was bred from the guanaco and the alpaca, kept for its luxury fibre, from the viçuna, which has the finest natural fibre in the world.

The llama can be found in two types, the Ccara and Tampuli, they are generally used as pack animals.

The huacaya alpaca looks like a cuddly 'teddy bear'.

The huacaya alpaca , with it's dense crimped fibre is the most popular in the UK.

Llamas are found in two types: Ccara and Tampuli. The larger Ccara is the one more usually seen in the United Kingdom. It has a short-to-medium length coat with short fibre on the legs and head. The Tampuli has a woollier coat with longer fibre reaching down the legs and often a woolly 'top knot'. There are also two types of alpaca: Huacaya and Suri. The 'teddy bear' Huacaya with its dense, crimped fibre is the most popular in the UK. The Suri has a silky coat which hangs down in long ringlets.

The British Llama Society and the British Alpaca Society exist to support members and promote these camelids. Anyone keeping either species is urged to join the appropriate breed society. Both societies operate a pedigree register and it is very strongly recommended that only registered animals be purchased. Advice is available from each society. The societies also offer assistance, particularly with welfare

The suri alpaca has a fine silky fleece that hangs down in ringlets.

Alpacas and llamas are herd animals and must never be kept on their own.

issues. Education courses, magazines, newsletters and social events enable owners to learn more about their animals and how to care for them. The charity British Camelids is supported by the breed societies and deals with camelid education and welfare.

Alpacas and llamas are naturally herd animals and must never be kept on their own. Alpacas can be stocked at 5–6 animals per acre and llamas at 4–5 animals per acre. Keeping two or three animals as pets or as guards for sheep and poultry is becoming increasingly popular. The animals rarely challenge fences and can be contained with 4-ft stock fencing, post-and-rail or electric-tape fencing. Electric netting should be avoided and all barbed wire removed. Where possible, grazing should be on a rotation basis and this must be considered when deciding how many animals can be kept. Paddocks should be free of toxic plants and of brambles, rye grass seeds and similar materials which can get tangled in the fleece. Any that does should be removed as soon as possible. Paddock cleaning is relatively easy since the animals tend to have specific soiling areas. They do not poach the ground and foot rot is not common but during lengthy wet periods, animals should be provided with access to an area of drier ground.

The breed societies offer opportunities to learn about camelids.

There should be a constant supply of fresh, clean water. A post-and-rail fence is sufficient to keep stock in the paddock.

Alpacas and llamas are hardy and can be kept outside year-round but they must be provided with shelter in the form of hedges, trees or purpose-built shelters. They must have sufficient grazing at all times with hay or haylage provided, particularly in winter, and a constant supply of fresh, clean drinking water. Supplemental concentrate feed should be given to pregnant and lactating females and to other animals in winter. Females are pregnant for around 11–11½ months and produce a single baby or cria.

Baby llamas and alpacas are known as cria.

Toe nails must be clipped regularly.

Ideally, animals should be checked twice daily to ascertain the 'normal' situation. Alpacas and llamas give little indication they are unwell and any unusual behaviour or symptoms of ill health can usually be detected during the daily check. Early help can then be given or veterinary assistance sought. Details of experienced camelid vets can be obtained from the British Camelid Veterinary Society.

A catch pen is useful for routine examinations which

include toe-nail clipping, vaccinations against clostridial diseases and worming. Vitamins A, D and E should be given during winter, especially to the cria. Teeth should be checked, with fighting teeth in young males being removed by a professional. Animals should be handled authoritatively but calmly and gently. They can be halter-trained, usually from about six months and llamas will carry loads and pull a cart.

Llamas do not require shearing. Their double fleece has coarse guard hairs covering a fine soft undercoat particularly sought by hand spinners. Huacaya alpacas are sheared annually with Suris sheared every other year. Both alpaca and llama fleece comes in a wide range of natural colours from white to fawn and brown to black. Fine alpaca fleece is used for a wide range of luxury products including yarn, jumpers, shawls, throws, coats and duvets. The lustrous silky Suri fibre is particularly suitable for blending with silk.

Camelids are hardy and can live outside all year round. They should be provided with shelter in the form of a hedge, trees or a field shelter.

Huacaya alpacas are sheared each year. Suri alpacas are sheared every two years and llamas do not require shearing.

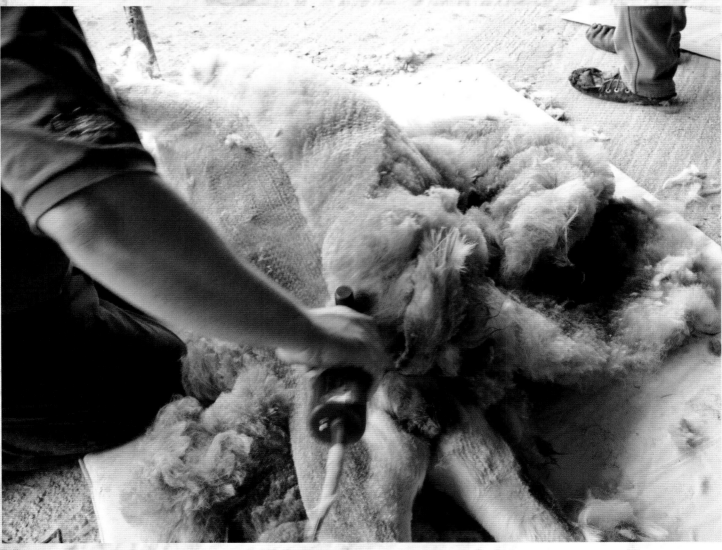

Shetland and Small Ponies

A small pony such as a Shetland can be kept on a half acre upwards but will need a companion of preferably another pony. The smaller the area of grassland, the cleaner it needs to be kept with droppings removed regularly. It may be possible to set aside an area to compost these for the garden. In wet weather the ponies will need to be confined in a large stable with a hard fenced outer area for exercise or they will cut up the grass and turn it to mud. Hay will need to be fed to supplement the grazing, probably all year round on a small area, and if working (perhaps being driven) the ponies will need some concentrate feed in the form of a mix or nuts. Clean water needs to be available all the time and shelter from bad weather and from the hot sun. Fly spray is necessary in the summertime. The ponies' hooves will need trimming but not necessarily shoeing if not doing road work, every eight weeks, and they will need a stringent worming programme and vaccinating for flu and tetanus plus regular dental checks.

Shetland ponies are tough and hardy, designed to live free in challenging conditions and some of them have strong characters so be sure you have enough knowledge to handle them. Miniature Shetlands are the smaller type in this breed but still with the Shetland characteristics. Miniature Horses are entirely different and are a scaled-down version of a thoroughbred type riding horse and should be a good example of this but in miniature. There are helpful societies for both breeds.

Donkeys

Donkeys are not small versions of ponies with long ears and shouldn't be treated as such.

They do require the same attention to the grassland

Shetlands put on weight very easily and are very much at risk from associated diseases such as laminitis. They need a balanced feeding regime but not over feeding or titbits.

Miniature horses are replicas of full sized horses and not shetlands. They have their own stud book and breed association and require knowledgeable management.

Donkeys are very prone to being overweight so lush grass is not advisable. They should have access to shelter at all times as their coats are not very waterproof.

To keep donkeys looking as happy and healthy as this one, watch they don't over eat and provide shelter at all times.

Some donkeys really suffer with biting flies and skin problems as a result. This fly rug is designed to fully protect the body from insects.

Is there anything prettier than a donkey foal? Although cute, they still need careful handling and training and of course, should be kept in pairs as they are herd animals.

but shelter is even more important for them as their coats are not hard and flat like ponies but almost fluffy and rain seeps through to their skin because they don't carry much natural grease. Also, because of their coats, they are more prone to external parasites such as lice and biting flies and need preventative treatment at appropriate times. Their hooves too are different in that their soles are thicker and need trimming accordingly. They are designed to live in hot, dry countries and walk over rocks to find limited food! Here they stand in wet fields and get plenty to eat making them prone to obesity. They should be fed barley straw, hay when there is little grass or during the winter, and a forage-based mix when extra feed is needed. They bond for life, should be kept in pairs and never separated. They can get a disease called hyperglycemias, which is an excess of lipids in the blood, which can be brought on by stress such as change of management, especially in overweight donkeys. They need regular foot care, dentals, worming and vaccinations.

Donkeys like human company but are strong so good handling is essential. They can be ridden but it's recommended that eight stone is the maximum weight for them to carry and they can be driven. Just a word of warning, the bray can be very, very loud and might be annoying to close neighbours!

Expanding your land

Living off your land is a satisfying experience and many people want to take it further beyond the confines of their garden. It's not always possible to move to a smallholding in the country, so what else can you do to increase your area?

Get an allotment

Local councils can provide land to be used for growing at a reasonable rent.

First approach your parish or town council for details of those in your area. The size varies but traditionally used to be a rood which is about a quarter of an acre. This then was divided during the last war into quarters to make a plot of ten poles. These days this often proves too much for gardeners who also have full-time jobs so half plots (five poles) and even smaller plots became available. Some areas continue to measure allotments in rods, poles and perches – not something you learn at school – but these all equate to about five metres. A chain is about 20 metres. It's very important not to take on an area that is too large for you to manage – you can always increase it at a later date. If there are no

allotments in your area you can look out of the area although it will mean travelling. Alternatively, look for like-minded people and approach your parish or town council. If there are at least six of you asking for plots, then under the 1887 Allotments Act, they are obliged to consider making provision. The other alternative is a privately owned allotment – perhaps your church has an unused field or a development has some wasteland.

An allotment will extend your land beyond the confines of your garden. Approach your parish or town council for information on provision in your area.

Allotments are particularly suitable for crops that like space such as a potato bed or the brassica family and will greatly extend the range of vegetables that can be grown.

What to look for in an allotment

In some areas you might be just grateful to get one but if you have a choice do consider the following points:

- How far is it from your home?
- Is it an easy journey – e.g. will crossing town take five minutes or an hour?
- Is the allotment site well kept?
- Do the fellow allotment holders seem friendly? (Visit on a weekend to see how they are running the site.)
- Is your proposed plot in good order or do you need to have a plan to clear it first?
- What sort of soil?
- Is water easily available?
- Are there any problems with vandalism? (This might not be something that stops people on this site but you may have to think in terms of taking all tools home and what crops to plant.)
- In your enthusiasm, think honestly about how long the plot will take to get right so you can grow vegetables and how long you have to do this. It might be a case of a lot of work initially and then more of a maintenance role.
- Are you allowed to keep tools at the site?
- Can you plant fruit trees and bushes?
- Can you keep poultry on site?

Having chosen your allotment, you then need to make a plan, taking into account factors like time, access to water, soil type, sun and shade, weeds and pests and availability of compost or manure. Start simply, with not too many crops. On the allotment you can grow the bigger vegetables that can't be easily fitted into containers or small gardens, such as brassicas, potatoes and root vegetables such as turnips, beetroot and carrots. Sweetcorn too is a possibility. Broad beans provide a delicious early vegetable. Soft fruit bushes may be useful to provide both fruit and some shade on your plot. The possibilities really are endless and trial and error is also a factor – keep notes and after a few years you will know what works on the allotment – but you no doubt will still have plenty of new ideas for the future!

Down on the city farm

The city farm movement grew out of increased community action from the 1960s and perhaps officially began with the first city farm being established in Kentish Town, London in 1972. In the USA the Community Garden movement provided inspiration for further developments as did the children's farm movement in the Netherlands. The number of city farms increased and is still increasing. Although the heaviest concentration of farms is in London, there are farms in most major cities now and in many suburbs. They do vary but usually do combine growing, often

City farms offer the experience to work with large farm animals within an urban setting. They offer opportunities for all ages and also for all levels of interest.

Visitors to city farms are able to buy produce from the farms while watching the animals and poultry that produced it.

For some visitors, City farms are about a green space in which children can play safely but for others they are where they can learn and practice farming and smallholding.

fruit and vegetables that represent the community in that area which makes for a fascinating experience, and livestock. Cattle, sheep, pigs and goats can be seen and handled in many inner city areas and because of their close proximity to people, become very tame. This means that people helping at city farms are able to really get to know each individual species perhaps in a way that they wouldn't be able to in a more traditional, extensive field setting. There is plenty of handling of livestock too which is very helpful if you are planning to keep stock yourself – even just finding out the size of different breeds is useful. Some farms also have horses

and ponies and run small riding schools – in fact some seriously competitive riders began their careers on a donkey at a city farm.

Poultry is usually a feature of city farms and many sell excess produce such as eggs and also make pickles and jams for sale. Every autumn there is a city farm harvest show where helpers bring the animals and produce and compete inter-farm for the coveted championship award. City farms allow urban and suburban dwellers to experience a range of stock and subsequently their management and also to learn new skills in both livestock and gardening.

Renting more land

Perhaps you have successfully reared orphan lambs and want to expand your sheep flock or maybe you want to try keeping other livestock. The next step is to look for a field or paddock to rent. It's often hard to find anything within a built-up area as "in-fill" planning has meant that most open spaces have been built on. Going out of town means that you not only want to find some land to rent but also somewhere reasonably safe for your livestock, so not on a main road if possible. Also sheep are very vulnerable to dog attacks. The ideal would be a field attached to someone's dwelling so there is someone keeping an eye on your stock when you are not there. As a general rule stock needs visiting twice a day, while breeding stock needs 24-hour attention when giving birth.

Good fencing means good friends and neighbours so any rented land has to have a safe boundary either erected by the landlord or, more usually, by yourself. The land also needs to have water or you will have to make arrangements to provide it on a daily basis. This will limit the number of animals you keep as during hot, dry spells, all livestock drink a surprisingly large amount and it's difficult to transport water. Look at the quality of the grazing or if you are planning to grow field crops, the soil type. Does it flood? Has it been overgrazed? What weeds are prevalent? Are there any poisonous plants that must be removed?

Rent does depend on which area you live in, the size of the field and the type of land. The landlord can

Good fencing means good neighbours. A fence that is safe and secure for livestock prevents not only injury to them but disputes with those whose land or gardens adjoin your paddock.

really set what he/she wants and you need to decide if the land is worth it to you. There should be a contract with notice either way especially if you have had to invest money putting up stock-proof fencing and, at the start, agree any individual requirements. With ponies and horses, there may be restrictions on grazing – they may want them removed for certain times of the year to rest the grazing or it is often part of the agreement that the droppings are picked up regularly. For other livestock there may be a stocking rate that you mustn't exceed (though never overstock anyway because it causes health problems). Happy renting means understanding and agreeing the terms and conditions on both sides and paying your rent regularly. Make sure there are no hidden extras such as paying water rates. Always keep the land in good order, not only for the sake of your animals or crops but also out of respect for the owner. Do not erect buildings without permission – in many areas planning permission from the local council is also needed.

Lots of people rent land for many years without any problems. By looking after the land and setting off with the basic requirements agreed, you have every chance of adding to your acreage on a long-term basis.

Many people welcome short term grazing by sheep on their land as it keeps the grass down and improves the growth if not overgrazed. Make sure the field is safe from dog attack.

To market, to market!

Whether buying or selling from a local market, they provide a forum where a range of fresh, local produce is on offer direct from the producers.

Farmers' markets

Once all markets were farmers' markets where local growers took their livestock and produce to be sold into the local area. Now food can travel thousands of miles (food miles), even being flown from Africa or Asia to reach supermarket shelves, providing out of season fruit, vegetables and flowers. But more and more people want to source locally and eat in season fruit and vegetables. If buying from farmers' markets, then the sellers will be able to tell you the complete history

Your local Community market can provide a good place to have a stall. These are usually run by your local Council and often encourage new stall holders.

At a Farmer's Market the producers of the goods are also the sellers so they are very knowledgeable about their produce and can tell customers how it was grown.

Many established markets really promote Farmer's Markets and Local Food. Go along and have a look at the stalls before approaching the Market Manager.

Plants and herbs are usually in demand and be prepared to speak about how to grow them on and cook them. Many buyers may be new to gardening.

of the food or flowers they are selling, maybe suggest recipes and tell you where it was produced. Fresh local food can supplement what you can grow yourself and give you ideas for future plans. If you have a surplus then these are good places to sell. They do have specified criteria which you need to meet so it's best to visit one first and see how they are organised, what equipment you would need, see what is already sold and check out the prices. Also, introduce yourself to the market manager and find out if there is space and what the charges would be. Other factors to consider are how you would present your produce – attractive marketing makes all the difference to sales. For example, an egg display might include a bowl of eggs with large photos of the free range flock behind.

If you decide that farmers' markets are for you then insurance is needed for product liability and public liability up to a recommended minimum of £5 million. You will also need to register with your local Environmental Health Officer (EHO) and follow any regulations relating to your particular foodstuffs. If selling any sort of cooked food such as jams, then expect the EHO to visit your premises, so find out their requirements. Although it seems a bit daunting, many small producers find farmers' markets an important source of income and also good fun. Speak to them to find out how they managed to start trading.

WI Country Markets
Another form of local market is the WI Country Markets. The WI or Women's Institute has always been

at the forefront of home baking and production and their markets are well known. There are 500 plus WI markets nationwide and they have the unique selling point of producing "home cooked" produce. Although you may still need to meet certain food hygiene regulations, this may be a slightly more informal way to get into market trading especially if your surplus is occasional. In 1995 the WI had to split their Country Markets away from the WI because the markets are seen as a business while the WI itself is a charitable organisation. The WI itself is keen to encourage new

Cooked food brings in a number of regulations including providing temperature controlled chilling cabinets and strict hygiene laws. Check these out at the start of your plans.

producers to the markets and has spent some time and money rebranding, promoting and updating the market's image including a brand new website. Visit your local WI market and see the range of produce that is on offer, the prices, and chat to the stallholders. Not only could you make some money from your produce but you will make new friends too.

Community markets

Up and down the country many traditional town and village markets are struggling against the competition of supermarkets and out of town shopping centres. These are not farmers' markets, often the goods come from far away such as cheap clothes or end of line cosmetics, but equally so, the vegetable and food stalls can and do feature local food.

Places near the sea tend to have fresh caught fish and shellfish and local delicacies such as samphire in East Anglia, UK, while locally grown potatoes and other fruit and vegetables feature on greengrocery stalls. Community markets are organised by the local council and stalls can be cheaper and more available than you might think, so it is well worth checking them out.

One of the very best methods of marketing any surplus produce is among your friends and family who will really appreciate the freshness and the fruits of your labours. Another good place is at your workplace and, subject to local council planning restrictions, you can put a small table outside your gate with an honesty box. Don't do this if it is dangerous for a car to pull in. Most likely you will find you cannot produce enough to keep up with demands of those close to you!

In it's simplest form, a stall can be outside your house. Permission might be necessary especially on busy roads but many Councils do turn a blind eye to seasonal stalls.

Meat and butchery carries a number of legal requirements from slaughter to sale. If you sell meat then you should also be able to talk about cooking methods and maybe have some recipes.

Grow your own vegetables

Not having a large or even medium sized garden will not restrict imaginative gardeners from growing a range of vegetables in the space that they have. These days seed companies are specifically producing seeds for patio and pot situations while windowsill gardening is becoming the norm with windowsill sized propagators being on sale.

Beginning with the smallest space, such as in a flat, windowsills or balconies (if you have one), become prime garden territory. Forget the colourful petunias and busy lizzies, these window boxes are going to be stuffed with salad leaves (cut and come again), herbs and strawberries and that's just for starters! Why wait for a greenhouse to grow tomatoes when the spare room windows provide perfectly good light and, stood on an old carpet, grow bags and pots are the same medium as a market gardener would use. You could even grow a container of new potatoes in a spare corner using one of the specially designed potato tubs or adapting your own. Sprouting seeds are not only tasty and varied but also extremely nutritious and using a seed sprouter takes up less than 20 sq cm and provides fresh, quick-growing sprouts. New varieties keep coming on the market – there's a lot more than mustard and cress now to choose, from including beans, garlic chives and alfalfa. For the more exotic,

Tomatoes are one of the most productive and rewarding crops that can be grown in a very limited area but it's worth learning how to trim them to get the best yield.

Lettuces and salad leaves are quick to germinate and to mature, growing almost anywhere it is warm and wet enough. Watch out for slugs and snails!

There are now so many varieties of tomatoes to choose from so it really is down to your taste. Cherry tomatoes can be very sweet while plums are firm but there are extra large ones too.

citrus fruit plants do bear fruit if the conditions are right, especially lemons. The rule is, if it will grow in a small space, then you can grow it on the windowsill, on the balcony or in a sunny room. The advantages are that crops are safe from pests (it's an ambitious slug that makes it to a high-level flat), you don't have to bend to tend them and the whole family can watch them grow.

Moving on to patios brings a whole new growing opportunity with container growing. Almost everything can be grown in pots provided they are large enough and situated in sun or shade depending on the plant's preference. But some vegetables are outstanding in pots. Lettuce and leaves of all types, from rocket to mizuna, lambs lettuce to purslane. Lettuce that hearts such as Little Gem is easily grown but the "cut and come again" type of salad leaves always please, have a longer growing span and are quite expensive in the shops. Tomatoes are the next obvious crop and two or three well fed plants that have their side shoots pinched out and their trusses controlled, will crop well throughout the summer. You can choose from cherry tomatoes, plums, beef steak or salad type fruits – or try two or three varieties. Cucumbers are also extremely willing to grow on sheltered patios – if open to inclement weather choose outside varieties and the gherkin plants not only provide tasty small cucumbers but usually have plenty over for pickling. Peppers too are very happy in a protected, pot situation and there are a huge number of varieties from the very hot to the salad pepper.

Less obvious crops in pots are peas and beans. The harvest is not huge (and stick to dwarf varieties) but they

Beetroot can be grown in large tubs and there are special varieties now that lend themselves to patio planting.

Although leeks grow very well in a small garden plot or on the allotment, smaller baby varieties can be container grown for a very tasty vegetable.

are quite quick growing and provide a wonderful fresh taste. Runner beans can crop quite well in containers – they are gross feeders and so they need large, deep containers that have plenty of nutrients. They will have to be supported against a wall, or more usually in a wigwam type arrangement of sticks. Go for the stringless varieties. Some are now being produced specifically for container growing. Swiss chard and spinach grow well in containers, the former providing colourful leaves while spinach provides an abundance of iron-rich leaves. Courgettes are quite happy in pots and there are the more unusual round varieties as well as the traditional shape. On the fruit side, top fruit, that is apples and pears for example, have been developed to provide a range of choice for container growing, even down to "family" trees where several different types of apples are grafted onto one root stock. Chose a self-fertilising variety. Dwarf cherry trees are another possibility while figs now are a common sight on patios.

Brassicas such as cauliflowers and cabbages are more suitable for larger plots and allotments though there are some varieties that are bred to grow in smaller spaces.

They may need winter protection with fleece. Soft fruit such as raspberries or blackberries grow well in tubs and you can protect them from birds by netting them when the fruit has set. Container fruit and vegetables are more dependent on the gardener than those planted out and it is up to you to ensure that they have sufficient but not too much water and that they are properly fed. They cannot produce fruit or vegetables if drowning, dehydrating or with no nutrients. It's a good start to growing in beds or on allotments because you really do get to understand what each type of plant needs to produce to the best advantage.

Don't forget vertical growing as well. Containers can be stood on stands to utilise height as well as floor space, or train cucumbers, beans and other trailing

Grow some baby carrots in raised beds or on a small plot for a real touch of luxury on your plate.

The more unusual vegetables such as this coloured cauliflower (Romenesco) are often difficult to find in supermarkets so why not grow your own!

plants up the wall or a trellis. Hanging baskets can be planted with tomatoes – in fact there are special trailing tomato varieties. Don't forget to feed them with the rest of the tomatoes. Trailing herbs do well in baskets too, such as thyme or mint. Don't let them dry out.

Raised beds are equally useful as part of a large or small garden. They also enable anyone who finds it hard to bend to be able to garden without discomfort. They are simply, confined areas of soil or compost raised off the ground and surrounded by boarding. Ready-made plastic or wood can be bought or you can make your own using wood to hand. Being raised, the drainage is good and you can control the nutrients within the bed depending on the crop. They won't need heavy digging either. By successional sowing, that is, sowing seeds at intervals throughout the growing season, you can ensure that you always have supplies of fresh vegetables and with more experience, you can extend the cropping season considerably.

A small greenhouse will considerably add to your choice of crops, your ability to raise seeds and extending the seasons. Some are barely walk-in, but a two metre by three metre greenhouse would enable the keen gardener to grow more exotic crops and give others a good start.

If you have a medium sized garden and can allow

even only a metre by two metres for growing outside vegetables, then you could grow runner beans, onions, sprouts, beetroot, parsnip and cabbage or cauliflower and plan it so early and late varieties keep you supplied from early summer to winter.

- Use every bit of space available – indoors as well as outdoors
- Feed container plants according to their needs
- Don't over or under water
- Choose varieties suitable for smaller spaces
- Plan successional sowing to provide a long growing season

- Experiment with different varieties – if unsuccessful find out why or don't grow them again!
- Grow your favourite vegetables
- If very limited stick to higher value vegetables such as salad leaves and tomatoes – you can grow a lot of these in the space a large cabbage would take
- Grow fun things like new potatoes for your Christmas dinner
- Involve the whole family

A well planned plot of only a metre by two metres can keep a whole family in fresh vegetables througout the growing season.

Working with wildlife

ildlife is everywhere and everything we do can affect what else is able to live in harmony with us. Urban areas have their own ecosystem and it's equally important in the country to improve and create habitats for a range of species.

The first step in improving conditions for wildlife is to identify what you already have. Keep a notebook of the birds you see, the insects and mammals and learn to identify them. Conserving wildlife doesn't just happen on the plains of a faraway country; we can play our part in our gardens whatever their size.

Bumblebees are well known to gardeners and a real sign of summer. There are 25 native species of bumblebees in the UK but already three have become nationally extinct with five on the UKBAP list and two more scheduled for inclusion. Numbers of the others are down. This is due to the loss of many traditional farming habitats and the increased use of pesticides, though now these are much more tightly controlled. So the bumblebee relies on the gardener. They get the most

Birds rely on habitat and a reliable food source in order to thrive. Try to provide both on your land and consider additional feeding in the winter.

Butterflies can be attracted by certain plants and flowers and learn to recognize the different caterpillars. Don't automatically kill them as some are now very low in numbers.

nectar from traditional cottage garden flowers and the least from annual bedding plants such as perlagoniums, begonias and busy lizzies. In early spring your fruit trees such as apple, cherry, pear and plum will attract them and then in early summer they enjoy thyme and chives (plus flowers such as wallflowers, campanulas, honeysuckle and single roses). Late summer they love lavender, mint and marjoram and are very attracted to sunflowers.

Providing a habitat too can help. Bumblebees like a dry, dark, ventilated cavity with a small entrance hole they can access at ground level. They are found in sheltered spots along a hedge or fence out of direct sunlight. You can also buy purpose-built bumblebee nests.

All birds and wildlife need somewhere to breed and shelter and food to eat. In the winter, leave leaves and sticks if they weren't cleared up early in the autumn, (but leave some anyway,) as by mid winter they will be shelter to insects and small mammals. If possible have some shrubs or a hedge to provide shelter for birds.

Leave some deadwood logs for beetles. Ivy is especially good, providing late autumn nectar for insects (and honey bees) and shelter and fruit for birds. If you have livestock though, keep it away from them.

Hedges and shrubs should not be trimmed during the nesting season from April to end of July and even then watch out for second broods.

Minimise the use of slug pellets and look for alternative methods. There are many of these, from copper rings to crushed egg shell or a tobacco solution. If you really have to use them, check the label very carefully for safety and remember that birds will eat the slugs that you have poisoned with the pellets and you need to be sure that this will not harm them. Slugs and snails are food for so many creatures, the fast disappearing song thrush, small mammals, toads and larger mammals such as urban foxes.

Three bumblebee species at least have become extinct and relies very heavily upon the nectar from flowers and habitat in the garden.

Bird feeding stations are a real life saver to birds in bad weather and increase the number able to breed. Hygiene is important though as birds can pass on diseases so keep them clean.

Consider having a bird feeding station but remember to regularly and thoroughly wash the containers as where birds gather together they are more likely to pass on disease to each other. In bad weather such as heavy rain or frosts, do put out some food for the birds as they will struggle to find it naturally.

Water features and ponds are great for wildlife and are used for drinking and for bathing birds while ponds encourage aquatic insects, dragonflies and frogs and toads to breed.

Keep a small patch of long grass to encourage insects for the birds.

Foraging for food

Wherever you live there will be wild food to be found. Wild blackberries grow everywhere and can be turned into delicious blackberry and apple pies in the autumn. Sloe berries make a warming winter sloe gin while elderberries and a huge range of berries and flowers can be made into wine. Even the humble nettle not only makes a lovely wine but also a very acceptable vegetable, tasting like spinach. Mushroom and fungi hunting can produce tasty results for the pan but take an expert or go on a course first as some fungi is very poisonous. Always check that it is legal to pick wild food and leave some for the future.

As you cultivate your plot, tend your animals or look for wild food, you will develop new skills and learn more and more about wildlife, birds and plants, plus becoming very aware of the daily weather. All those working with the land in any form keenly feel the turn of the seasons and the year becomes an exciting adventure of discovery; the first buds, the first flowers, the first vegetables, the smell of a thunderstorm, the crispness of the first frosts and the flutter of the snow. Growing your own food opens up your world in more ways than one.

Elderberries are the symbol that autumn have arrived and can be made into a warming wine or syrup for colder winter days. Birds love them too and form part of their survival kit.

A number of insects find nettles useful but humans too can enjoy the taste. Young nettle tops are similar to spinach and they make a good wine or even beer too.

Index

Acknowledgements

The Publisher would like to thank the following people and organisations for their kind help and contribution:

Gorse Hill City Farm, *Leicester, UK*
Rupert Stephenson Poultry and Wildlife Collection, *UK*
Chris Greenwood at Poultry Park, Gloucester, *UK*
Shaun Hammon at The Wernlas Collection, *Shropshire, England*
Sarah and Callum Foulks, *Oswestry, UK*
Frank Lane Picture Agency, *Suffolk, UK*
Emma and Shane Durston, *Lincolnshire, UK*
Ron and Beryl Bramhall, *Maesbrook, Shropshire, UK*
Colin Hughes, The Shropshire Smallholders Group, *Shropshire, UK*
Carol Meaden - for allowing us to photograph her Quail - *Oswestry, UK*
Hoo Farm, Telford, *Shropshire, UK*
Buzzwords Editorial Ltd, Kettering, *Northamptonshire, UK* for contributing the
articles and pictures on Bees and Camolids.

Special thanks from the Author:

Thank you to Janice Houghton Wallace, Secretary of the Turkey Club of
Great Britain for her contribution on turkeys. Smallholder Magazine,
Federation of City Farms and Gardens, Poultry Club of Great Britain, British
Waterfowl Association, the Donkey Sanctuary, Sidmouth, Michael Knight,
Buffy and all the livestock and poultry that have given me so much
pleasure and the knowledge to write this book.

Special photography courtesy of Mirco De Cet